D0450102

B   Mearns
Lincoln   Largely Lincoln

600

STORAGE

SAN DIEGO PUBLIC LIBRARY

LIBRARY RULES

TIME: — Books may be kept 14 days, unless dated otherwise.

RENEWALS: — Books may be renewed once at the agency where borrowed, unless on reserve. Bring book with you.

FINES: — Five cents a day will be charged for each ~~adult~~ book kept overtime, ~~two cents a day for each juvenile book.~~

DAMAGES: — *Injury to the book from tearing, penciling, unusual soiling or other ill-usage, will be charged to the card owner. Please report to us when a mutilated book is issued to you.*

CARDS—ALWAYS BRING YOUR CARD WITH YOU.

LARGELY LINCOLN

B
LINCOLN

LARGELY LINCOLN

by

David Chambers Mearns

INTRODUCTION BY

EARL SCHENCK MIERS

SAN DIEGO PUBLIC LIBRARY

St Martin's Press
NEW YORK

Copyright © 1961 by David Chambers Mearns
All rights reserved
Library of Congress Catalog Card Number: 61–7889
Manufactured in the United States of America
by H. Wolff, New York

Some of the pieces in *Largely Lincoln* first appeared in periodicals in the United States. *Big Day in Ottaway* was published in the *Washington Post;* Journal of the New Jersey Historical Society published *Who in Triumph Advances; More Portentous Sound* appeared in the Simmons College Books and Publications; *Scalping of Abraham Lincoln* appeared, in part, in the *Journal of the Illinois State Historical Society* and in part, in the *Journal of the Manuscript Society.* The author wishes to thank the editors of those magazines for permission to reprint the pieces here. He wishes to thank, also, the Association of College Research Libraries for permission to print the speech, *In the Presence of the Schollars.*

FEB 19 1962

FOR WORTH AND WALTER

Introduction

W H A T frightful folly it would be for me to recall the time, now long years agone, when I first met David C. Mearns. I know that it was a happy occasion, filled with laughter and warm-hearted conversation, and that I came away a wiser man; but in this sense I am always meeting David Mearns for the first time, for he possesses that rare gift of ageless companionship which, though the years may stiffen muscles, leaves the spirit nimble and the heart unburdened. Such a fellow must have been A. Edward Newton, the only other bibliophile-essayist, in my opinion, who deserves to slam out metaphors in the same literary league with Dave Mearns. The figure is not as strained as you may think; reading, like baseball, is a spectator sport and once each generation along comes a practitioner of the game who simply outshines the field. After you have read the real part of this volume—Mr. Mearns' part—you will know exactly what I mean.

A book like this stands apart, a piece of great luck to humanity, for the reason that no one could plan it. Such a book has to tumble out by the merest chance because now and then, in the pressure of getting and taking, life produces an individual endowed with the gentler and worthier capacities of a scholar. In the judgment of heaven, he must be the world's only genuine realist—this man above the grubby plunder of the fortune-seeker who, probing for truth, is sweetened by the compassion that becomes the merry handmaiden of such enterprise. There is always an unmistakable twinkle in the clear eyes of this kind of man; and like Tennyson, frequenting The Cock, that excellent tavern on the north of Temple Bar, there is in him always a buoyancy toward his fellow man:

> *O plump head-waiter at the Cock,*
> *To which I most resort,*
> *How goes the time? 'Tis five o'clock—*
> *Go fetch a pint of port.*

With this kind of man there come golden moments when the twinkle flashes, when the tale he has been pursuing is too good any longer to keep to himself, and the minutes slip away on wings of enchantment. Of such moments is this book compounded; to plan it, one must live it first.

For David Chambers Mearns that experience began a mite more than sixty years ago in Washington, D. C. when McKinley still occupied the White House. From blue-eyed toddler to rangy teen-ager, Dave followed the pattern of sturdy growth that nature reserves for boys and weeds; and the image of his home town—Lafayette Square in the spring, the bustle of Pennsylvania Avenue, the gentle slopes of the Hill—became a first love in his heart. The irrepressible Teddy Roosevelt exploded upon the city, to be succeeded by jolly Big Bill Taft, who sweated out his four unwanted years in the Executive Mansion, and then the sober Wilson arrived to make the world safe for democracy and Calvin Coolidge. By then David Mearns had begun his more than forty years of service with the Library of Congress, and precisely how Mr. Coolidge made his own unique contribution to our young hero's education during these formative years comprises the illuminating and often hilarious essay with which this collection concludes.

The now legendary Herbert Putnam was the Librarian of Congress when Mearns began his career within those marbled halls. A more perceptive tutor no young bookman could have found; a man of genius, of force and of remarkable capabilities, wonderfully gentle, deeply sensitive, Putnam remade the Library of Congress into his own lengthened shadow. His "fortunate impress," Archibald MacLeish said of Putnam in later years, was "upon everything he touched"—including, for the benefit of future American scholarship, the mind and spirit and personality of David Chambers Mearns.

Among Putnam's invaluable creations was the Library's Manuscript Division, housed today on the third floor of the Library of Congress Annex and containing in its stacks some 16,000,000 items that range across every facet of American life. Under the modest title of "Chief," David Mearns has for ten years presided over this great treasure house of national culture, not as a remote administrator lost in details of cataloguing but as a scholar's scholar believing the Manuscript Division is a resource existing for the use of the nation's historians. Some months ago I wrote in the magazine *History,* anent the Manuscript Division and its Chief: "Whether a scholar's labors carry him into the still little used papers of the American Colonization Society or into the mass of documents of the League of Women Voters so popular with students of the current political scene, each is serving the national culture with equal passion. Each needs help, sympathy, appreciation, and a loyal friend, the qualities that make Dave Mearns a national institution among historians." Certainly it is no accident that he also holds the chair of history, which was attached to the division through an endowment from William Evarts Benjamin of the same state that produced the great hair collector of another essay in this volume.

Although the vitality of home-town Washington, the inspiration of bookman-mentor Herbert Putnam, and the exciting flow of history under the eleven Presidents who have dwelt in the White House during the past six decades have left their marks upon David C. Mearns, none has quite been the Great Teacher. This distinction belongs, really, to that "Tall Sucker" from Springfield, Illinois, who said so simply of his own background: "Education, defective." Perhaps the past century has produced other students of the life and times of Abraham Lincoln who have equaled Mearns' everlasting diligence in combing the record for the truth; and there may even be a few who are his peer in intimate understanding of the soul and purpose of Mr. Lincoln; but none has gained more from his labors. "The son of a gun grows on you," Mearns writes of Lincoln, quoting Carl Sandburg; and over a rich and busy lifetime he has pursued his happy quest of learning of, and from, the "long black fellow" (the phrase is Lincoln's) who rode out of the Illinois prairies to hold together a divided nation.

The larger part of this volume reflects that quest. Much of what is revealed will come as a delightful surprise, rewarding the reader with fresh insight into Lincoln and his age. Yet what pupil, aspiring to be a historian, could have had a better instructor than one who believed, as Mr. Lincoln said to Judge Douglas in the debate at Jonesboro, "I do not state a thing and say I know it when I do not. . . . I mean to put a case no stronger than the truth will allow."

In the spirit of these words, David Mearns explores byways in history from which others have shrunk. How reliable were the memories of those who in life claimed to have known the "Saint of Sangamon"? To this query, in his opening essay, Mr. Mearns brings into play the marvelous skill of the scholar-turned-detective, which of course is the essence of competent research. In "The Constant American" he employs the same gift in sorting through hundreds of documents in the Lincoln Papers so that the reader "can behold Mr. Lincoln's America and see standing among them America's Mr. Lincoln." The sheer fun that so often emerges from such toil shines through "The Scalping of Abraham Lincoln"—ah, what profits slipped through the fingers of the Great Emancipator's barber! Quickly David Mearns can become entirely serious as he traces the meaning of Mr. Lincoln to our Canadian friends ["Lincoln and the Image of America"]; and in his "Great Day in 'Ottaway'" and "Who in Triumph Advances" he brings to the events of history—the beginning of the Lincoln-

Douglas debates and the President-elect's seven hours in politically hostile New Jersey—the full force of fresh material and new dimension.

Often the mood changes: there is deep tenderness in "Abraham Lincoln as a Purer Nelson," a note of impishness in the President's "adventure" with that remarkable charmer known as the Princess Salm-Salm, and a profound investigative impulse to the story of Mr. Lincoln and the theater that adds much to our sum of knowledge. And there is more—quite properly is this volume entitled *Largely Lincoln,* for it is concerned chiefly with the student's discovery of why his Great Teacher was so intrinsically a man of the ages.

Yet there are occasional side excursions that provide equal pleasure. We dare say the Madison Avenue phrase-maker does not exist who can believe he has contributed as much as he thought to American culture once he has encountered D. P. Gardner, the New England Soap Man; and that weary tribe of bleary-eyed readers known as genealogists will find in "The Infatuate Wish" more comfort than librarians usually bestow on them. But enough of my rambling; in an earlier age Lincoln had another great admirer named Walt Whitman who said so much better all that I have tried to say:

Camerado, this is no book,
Who touches this touches a man.

EARL SCHENCK MIERS

Edison, New Jersey
February, 1961

Contents

LARGELY LINCOLN

The Inexhaustible Story

WASHINGTON in the District of Columbia is a Lincoln village. If any doubt the statement let them look to their telephone directory. There a man may dwell in the Lincoln Apartments, lunch at the Lincoln Cafe, tipple at Lincoln Liquors, array himself from Lincoln Clothiers, send his wife to the Lincoln Clinic for Women and treat her with medications from the Lincoln Drug Company, decorate his home from the Lincoln Furniture Company, fill his larder from the Lincoln Market, purchase sundries from the Lincoln Five and Ten Cent Store, borrow money from the Lincoln Loan Company or deposit it in the Lincoln Bank, find diversion in the Lincoln Theater and at last seek eternal rest in the Lincoln Memorial Cemetery.

There can be no doubt about it; in Washington Mr. Lincoln has attained celebrity; indeed, he appears to be inescapable; a vast literature records his tenancy of the White House. Insofar as it relates to his conduct of the Presidential office, to his transactions as Head of State, to his exchange of correspondence with other prominent personages, it is reasonably full and often approaches redundancy. But, with respect to his *private* life and the activities of the lesser participants in the Lincoln story it is meager, conflicting, and confusing. This is because our knowledge of those aspects has derived largely from reminiscence set down long after the episodes and incidents had actually transpired. Memory, I would remind you, memory is sometimes perverse, sometimes subversive, sometimes capricious and sometimes frenziedly fantastic. Moreover, for a generation, there was a little group of men who earned their livelihoods by remembering Mr. Lincoln. The more they concentrated on their subject, the more they remembered, and whenever they found themselves in want or in straightened circumstances, they would quite providentially remember something else. On the fringes of this coterie, was another company of gentlemen who, in later life, delighted to regale their heirs and other captive guests with detailed recitals of their intimate knowledge of the Saint from Sangamon. I do not impugn the credibility and honor of these worthies, but I *do* suggest that there may have been instances where a spurious sense of history has suborned the witness. Because of that possibility and because of the rarity of total recall—always excepting tainted geniuses of television—modern scholarship insists on contemporary evidence. Reminiscence, when not disdainfully dismissed, is set aside as not proved; it cannot answer questions; it can only raise them.

By way of illustration, let me cite an article in a recent issue of the *Lincoln Herald,* written by Mr. Joseph George, Jr., and entitled "The Night John Wilkes Booth Played Before Abraham Lincoln." Mr. George cautiously and correctly states that Mr. Lincoln was in the audience at Ford's Theatre on Monday evening, November 9, 1863, when John Wilkes Booth played his dual role of "Phidias" and "Raphael" in *The Marble Heart*. In making the statement Mr. George has the contemporary evidence of John Hay's *Diary* to support him. But the *New York World* for April 19, 1865, and the *Philadelphia Press* for the following day, published a report by George Alfred Townsend—the redoubtable "Gath"—which declared:

The personal relations existing before the murder between Booth and the President, augment the horror of the occurrence. Mr. Lincoln saw Booth play more than once, and particularly admired him. He once applauded him rapturously, and with all that genial heartiness for which he was distinguished . . . The President had never spoken with Booth, but wished to make his acquaintance, and said so.

Again, Mr. George quite properly rejects the Townsend story on the ground that "none of Mr. Lincoln's associates ever left an account of the incident." But for my own part, I am not so much troubled because the Townsend assertion is probably false as I am because it may possibly be true. Earlier in 1863, Booth had been in Washington for some weeks, and that stay deserves more careful study than it has so far received. For him who will assume that research I submit a few points and, perhaps, point a moral or two to boot.

The engagement began on Saturday, April 11, when the *Daily Morning Chronicle* announced:

John Wilkes Booth.—This accomplished young actor makes his first appearance at Grover's theater to-night. Mr. Booth is a son of J. B. Booth, a younger brother of Edwin Booth, and may be said to inherit much of his father's ability and talent. Indeed when we have seen him in some of those old Shakespearean plays in which his father was so renowned, we have almost thought that the elder Booth was before us, and have been carried back to the days of our early play-going, when J. B. Booth was to our mind the real Richard, and the illusion was so complete that we involuntarily paid to him the homage belonging to a king. None of the younger Booths so often remind us of the great tragedian, their father, as John Wilkes. Edwin will doubtless be claimed by the critics the better actor, but in our judgment John exhibits more of those peculiar qualities which distinguished his great father, who had no superior and rarely an equal, upon the American or English stage. John Wilkes is a very young man, but he has sprung at once to fame solely upon his own merits, and not upon any factitious fame which belonged to his great father.

Billed as "the youngest 'star' in the world," he seems to have given a satisfactory performance. A reviewer wrote:

John Wilkes Booth.—Last evening, this popular and talented young tragedian made his *debut* in this city, and was greeted by a brilliant and fashionable audience, who testified their appreciation of his merits by the most unbounded applause. Mr. Booth though several years younger than his brother Edwin, bears a most striking resemblance to him, not only in his personal appearance, but even the tone of his voice is very similar. Our recollection of the latter in the character of the Duke of Gloster is vivid—and we believe it is considered one of his favorite parts—and it is difficult to determine which of the brothers excels in their representation of the bloodthirsty and haughty monarch.

Thus far the reports are contemporaneous, but when, in 1885, Alexander Hunter's *New National Theatre, Washington, D. C.: A Record of Fifty Years* was published, it contained this passage:

On Saturday, April 11, 1863, the announcement is made that the distinguished young actor, John Wilkes Booth, will make his first appearance in Washington as "King Richard III." A very large and fashionable audience greeted him, and, a singular coincidence, President Lincoln and Senator Oliver P. Morton occupied a private box.

Mr. Lincoln had returned to Washington only the night before after having visited Hooker's Army at Falmouth.

Surely, Mr. Hunter had *some* authority for placing Mr. Lincoln at the play, and yet, what his source was, I have not yet discovered. It was given on a Saturday, and most of the Washington papers did not publish Sunday editions at that time. The *Chronicle* was an exception; it reported only (as I have said) that the audience was "brilliant and fashionable." It may have been put early to bed. The fact that Morton was then not a Senator but the Governor of Indiana may be excused as a minor lapse. When we ask ourselves, if the opportunity had presented itself, would Mr. Lincoln have attended *Richard III,* it is easy to find an affirmative: On August 17 of that year, Mr. Lincoln wrote to James H. Hackett, another thespian, "I should like to hear you pronounce the opening speech of Richard the Third," and on March 2, 1864, Mr. Lincoln himself pronounced the lines in the presence of Francis Bicknell Carpenter, the portraitist. But Mr. Lincoln certainly did not attend Booth's performance on the evening of April 11, 1863, and, in consequence of contrary and contemporary evidence, Mr. Hunter's explicit statement may be explicitly dismissed. The *Evening Star* contemporaneously established Mr. Lincoln's alibi, reporting that he had attended the Washington Theatre at the cor-

ner of Eleventh and C Streets where he saw Mrs. John
Wood as Pocahontas and had laughed visibly and audibly
at the burlesque.

But Booth's Washington appearance in the spring of
1863 deserves careful attention for another reason. It will
be remembered that, at the request of certain officials of
the Government, Dr. John Frederick May, of Washington, was, in 1865, called upon to identify Booth's body.
This he did by recognizing a scar on Booth's neck. Long
afterward, specifically in January, 1887, he wrote out his
reminiscences of the episode, under the title of *The Mark
of the Scalpel*, which was finally published in the *Records*
of the Columbia Historical Society in 1910. Permit me to
quote a paragraph from the original manuscript now in
the Library of Congress:

Some time before the assasination of President Lincoln, a
fashionably dressed, and remarkably handsome young man
accompanied by a friend, entered my office in Washington,
and introduced himself to me as Mr. Booth. After some ordinary conversation, he told me, "he was playing an engagement
with Miss Charlotte Cushman, and was much annoyed by a
large lump on the back of his neck, which for some time past
had been gradually increasing in size, and had begun to show
above the collar line of the ordinary theatrical costume." He
said, "he wished to have it removed;" and he particularly enjoined me to say, (if questioned upon the fact of his having
undergone a surgical operation), "that it was for the removal
of a bullet from his neck." But he did not give any reason for
this request. Without promising to observe this injunction, I
examined his neck, and found on the back of it, and rather on
the left side, quite a large fibroid tumor, but which could
have no connection with a bullet, as to its origin, or in any

other way. I advised its removal but at the same time told him, I would take it out on one condition, which was, "that he should suspend his engagement at the theatre, and observe absolute rest." He replied, "he did not wish to do this, in fact, he could not." I then explained to him the importance of his remaining quiet after such an operation upon the ground of his personal appearance, "that there were two principal ways, by which a wound made by a surgical operation healed. The first, and most to be desired, by primary adhesion, by which, if the edges were brought closely together, and kept in contact for some little time, they became directly united, and left so fine a line of cicatrix, as scarcely to be noticed. But this bond of union, though daily becoming stronger, was weak for some days after the adhesion, and could easily be broken by undue violence; and once broken, the wound would gape, and its edges not be likely to re-unite; and then the space between them would have to fill up with new tissue or flesh, and an ugly scar would be left." After quietly listening to his explanation, he told me in a very decided way he "could not stop playing his engagement; but would be very careful in acting, and moderate his movements, so as to make no strain on the wound." I saw it was necessary to humour him; for there was so much determination in his manner, as to convince me, he had decided to have the offending object at once removed, and whatever might be the result, he would himself become responsible for it. Compromising with him then upon that basis, I removed it. The wound perfectly united by the primary or direct process, and I congratulated him upon the slight scar that would be left. But in about a week after it had united, he came one morning to my office, with the wound torn open and wide gaping, and told me, "that in some part of the piece he was playing with Miss Cushman, she had to embrace him, and that she did so with so much force, and so roughly, that the wound opened under her grasp." The indirect and tedious course of healing, by granulation, now followed, and left a *large and ugly scar*.

Dr. May prided himself on having been "particular in giving the details of this conversation." Indeed, he went so far as to place the dialogue in quotation marks; thus bespeaking a tape-recording ear and an infallible memory. But, strangely, he did not state when the operation was performed, contenting himself by saying only that it took place "some time before the assassination of President Lincoln." Fortunately the date can be supplied by reference to a contemporary newspaper. The *Daily National Republican* for April 17, 1863, announced:

Benefit of J. Wilkes Booth.—Grover's Theatre.—This evening two of the most popular of Shakespeare's plays, the "Merchant of Venice," and the "Taming of the Shrew." Mr. Booth is a young man of rare abilities, and, considering his experience, really wonderful in his impersonations. His representations, notwithstanding the severe surgical operation of Monday evening last, entitle him to the admiration of the public.

Thus it would seem clear that Booth paid his first visit to Dr. May's office on April 13, 1863.

But Charlotte Cushman was not playing at Grover's at that time. Susan Denin was the leading lady of the company. As a matter of fact, Miss Cushman gave only a single professional appearance at Washington during Mr. Lincoln's occupancy of the Executive Mansion: that was on October 17, 1863, and Booth was not in the cast. These slips in the Doctor's story make more curious and mysterious, the Doctor's report of Booth's injunction to him that, if questioned on the nature of the operation, he should say "that it was for the removal of a bullet from his neck."

If it was not for that purpose, we must ask ourselves what had become of Booth's bullet. There are several versions of how and where he came by it. For example, the New York *World*, on April 17, 1865, published this account:

Upon the strength of his father's name he [Booth] managed to secure various engagements in the South and West. One of these was made with Mr. Matthew Canning, lessee of the theater at Montgomery, Alabama. While acting there, Wilkes, becoming involved in a quarrel on one occasion, was shot in the neck. The ball remained imbedded in the flesh for a period of perhaps two years, and came out unexpectedly during his first engagement at Grover's Washington Theater, in the Spring of 1863.

Stanley Kimmel tells the story in these words:

At the close of the Richmond season Wilkes played short engagements elsewhere before returning north for the summer . . . The reopening of stage doors took him back south where he tried stardom, under the name of J. Wilkes, at Matthew Canning's Columbus (Georgia) Theatre. The night he was to play Hamlet another actor was with him in his dressing room when Canning entered and jokingly threatened to shoot both of them. The gun unexpectedly exploded and Wilkes "was shot in the rear." This accident kept him off the stage for several weeks.

Matthew Canning's name appears in both of these relations. Mr. Canning was in Philadelphia on April 15, 1865, when he was arrested on orders from the Provost Marshal General. On his person was found a manuscript biography of Booth, presumably in Canning's hand. It read in part:

In the season of 1859 he [Booth] made his first appearance as a Star in Columbus, Ga., the Theatre there being under the managment of a gentleman from this City, who during the first week of his engagement, accidentally shot Booth in the side: After his recovery he made his appearance under the same management in Montgomery, Ala., where he played a highly successful engagement.

But Mr. Canning was still Booth's manager in April, 1863, and was in Washington when Booth went to see Dr. May. He may have been the friend who accompanied Booth to the doctor's office. In any event, it seems reasonable to suppose that Canning knew the location of the wound, its cause, and the consequence of the operation.

As I have said, Mr. Canning was arrested the day Lincoln died. He was sent to Washington where he was confined in the Old Capitol Prison and finally released upon taking the oath of allegiance. It was during his involuntary absence from Philadelphia that Mr. E. D. Saunders, President of the Veterans Bounty Fund Commission, wrote to General Fry: the Provost Marshal General:

The Government, it is understood, has arrested Matthew Canning of this City. The father-in-law, Mr. G. R. Johnson, a most worthy citizen, residing in Camden, loyal & patriotic, with the wife of Canning, an estimable lady, will call on you.

She said that her husband accidentally shot Booth; and the wound, as her husband informed her, has left a large scar on his person, not to be mistaken when once described. Perhaps this may be known to the authorities.

In the light of so many discrepancies how much credibility can be placed in Dr. May's memory and his mark of the scalpel? I have recounted the episode only to illustrate the fact that the Lincoln story is inexhaustible; that much fresh work needs to be done; and that ancient witnesses should be cross-examined and occasionally impeached.

The Constant American

SECRETARY STANTON was not given to prophecy but when he said that Lincoln "belongs to the ages," he spoke the truth. He *is* one of us. He *is,* as he has been in every generation, a public utility and a national resource. He is torn from the context of *his* own time and projected without consent or consideration into ours. He deserves a better break. His modernity (it seems to me) is unbecoming not of him but of us. We can say that the fault is his.

And we can wonder at the literature which confines him; wonder how he could, at once appeal, as subject, to Horatio Alger and Earl Browder, to an English nobleman and a German opportunist, to a poet and a chiropodist. We can wonder at his successors who, in moments of national travail and personal perplexity, have looked out from his window upon the White House lawn and found solution and comfort and assurance by asking "What would Lincoln do?" We can wonder at an elderly woman, in a Japanese prison camp on the island of Sumatra, who through months of captivity secreted on her person a letter from Mr. Lincoln to her grandfather. We can wonder why credulous journalists continue to ask what Mr. Lincoln's course of action would be, were he confronted with this or that present crisis. We can wonder why so few of his followers are women. We can wonder how he looked and how he sounded when he laughed.

And we can beguile ourselves with futile speculation and one man's guess will be as satisfactory or as unsatisfactory as another's. And we can be thankful that we who know so much of him, have yet so much to learn. But although Mr. Lincoln belongs to the saints of a latter day, he is, I suspect, a most reluctant contemporary. For there was about him a reality which our powers of enraptured embellishment cannot quite destroy, dissemble, or defy, and if he belongs to the ages it is because he belonged inseparably to his own age, his own fellows, his own environment. Removed from them he becomes an unhappy fantasy, and, what is worse, he becomes ridiculous. For he was the participant of a time and only as its participant has he come to timelessness. Because this is so, it is as fatuous as it is idle, to require him to share *our* world. On the contrary, if we would honor, recognize and understand him we must return to *his*. Perhaps we can, with old companions as our guides. Here is one:

First time I saw Lincoln was when he came down Sangamon River from Macon Co. in a canoe—He was as ruff a specimen of humanity as could be found. . . . diffidence and generosity were the causes of his failing to accumulate anything during early life.

And here is another witness of those New Salem days:

Lincoln had nothing only plenty of friends. His pants were made of flax and low, cut tight at the ankle—his knees were

both out. Was the roughest looking man I ever saw—poor
boy, but welcome to everybody's house. . . . Bargain with
Mrs. Nancy Miller was this—was to maul 400 rails for each
yard of brown jeans dyed with white walnut bark, until he
got enough to make a pair of pants. God never made a finer
man than Abraham Lincoln! Need not be with a man more
than an hour to gain his good will.

And here is another one:

Met Lincoln at New Salem 1830, was Capt. of Flatboat—
Boat belonged to Denton Offut—[Lincoln] was standing on
mill dam trying to pry boat off—pants rolled up about a foot,
dressed very ruff—blue jeans breeches, a hickory shirt—alter-
nate stripes of white and blue—made of cotton . . . Whenever he could find a young man he put him on right course,
encouraged morality, integrity and honesty. . . . Was always
appointed one of judges when at horse race and was never objected to by either party.

And here is yet another:

When I first saw Lincoln he was lying on a trundle bed
rocking a cradle with his foot—was almost covered with
papers and books—There was one half foot space between
bottom of pants and top of socks.

And another still:

When he began to study law he would go day after day for
weeks and sit under an oak tree on hill near Salem, and read
—moved round tree to keep in shade—was so absorbed that
people said he was crazy.

A former partner described him this way:

There are no sticking points in his history—Growth was
steady, gradual and constant. . . . Better at defending and

improving existing systems than in originating—Does not believe in reforming so much as perfecting.

Young Matthew Marsh wrote to his family from New Salem:

The Post Master Mr. Lincoln is very careless about leaving his office open & unlocked during the day—half the time I go in & get my papers, etc. without anyone being there as was the case yesterday . . . luckily he is a very clever fellow & a particular friend of mine. If he is there when I carry this to the office—I will get him to frank it.

Mr. F. M. Wright, of Urbana, Ohio, wrote to President-elect Lincoln:

. . . Now my Dear Abe, if you have any old Shoes, Boots, Pants indeed any article of clothing suitable for a *growing* family—will be acceptable—especially shirts or under cloathing of any Kind, for I desire to get as near to your *hide* as I can—I feel *"Irrepressible"* love springing up in my heart. . . . Send by express.

It is these elements which give such transcendent importance to the Lincoln Papers. They are phrased in the vernacular which came so readily to his tongue. They are simple. They are alive and they communicate their liveliness. From them we can behold Mr. Lincoln's America and see standing among them America's Mr. Lincoln. There he is with his fellows. If we would know him we must know them too.

The Scalping of
Abraham Lincoln

IT HAS long been one of my minor ambitions to be widely
recognized and heralded as *the* authority on some personal
characteristic of Abraham Lincoln. Unhappily, the field
is constantly narrowing. Phrenologists and sculptors have
claimed and captured for themselves the right to publish
learned monographs on the bony structure of his cranium.
Ophthalmologists and the late Franklin Knight Lane have
reserved to themselves the privilege of discoursing on his
eyes. Dermatologists have insisted that the wart upon his
upper lip is *their* exclusive province. In consequence and
somewhat hurriedly, I must announce myself as *the* Spe-
cialist on Mr. Lincoln's hairesy.

In this life-work, I acknowledge the encouragement
given by my ancient companion, Daniel Druff. He has expressed a hope that I will continue my explorations of the
place of hair in history. There is, he believes, a chance to
do for hair what Admiral Mahan did for sea power. By
way of bibliographical sources he suggests: William Somerset Maugham's *The Razor's Edge;* George Meredith's
The Shaving of Shagpat; Alexander Pope's *Rape of the*

Lock; Earl Derr Brigger's *Seven Keys to Baldpate;* Alice Hegan Rice's *Mrs. Wiggs of the Cabbage Patch;* Rossini's *Barber of Seville;* Browning's *Parting at Morning;* almost anything written by Edmund ("the unspeakable") Curll; and that old but ever popular ballad, *Woan Gillette Me Call You Sweetheart.* This by way of introduction and apology.

It has not been ascertained that Mr. Lincoln, who professed to love him and to follow him into the most exalted realms of Whiggery, ever read the letter which Henry Clay addressed more than a century ago to the notorious Mr. Edward Phalon of New York City. That imperishable document was, as everyone knows, subsequently published in Manuel J. Vieira's *The Tonsorial Art Pamphlet: Origin of the Trade, The Business in America and Other Countries, Its Rise and Progress,* Indianapolis: Publishing House Print, 1877. Among its lofty expressions (*vide* p. 11) are these familiar lines:

I . . . thank you for the bottle of your invigorator which you had the goodness to send me. I will give it a fair trial. Although in advanced age nothing can avert the appearance of gray hair and wrinkles and other evidences of lapse of years, it is well enough to put on and preserve our good looks as well and as long as we can. From the favorable account of your Invigorator, I think it must contribute to the object of your success and prosperity in life.

For the fur-bearing Mr. Lincoln, a man prodigal of follicle, this message would probably have been of sentimental interest only; for, when it came to hair, he was, like Nancy, his mother, a creature of Hanks.

When Frederick F. Hassam (Childe Hassam's father),

a precise New England merchant and antiquary, came to Washington in the summer of 1861, he arranged, through Charles Sumner, to see the President. An appointment was made. Mr. Hassam's account of the interview, published in *The Brooklyn Standard Union*, October, 1900, conveys some exciting information:

　　The thermometer at midday was 110, atmosphere very sultry, hot. I think it was the hottest day I ever experienced. Mr. Lincoln was in deshabille in his private room upon the second story of the White House. His whole attire consisted of a white shirt, open front, black trousers, common low slippers called by shoe men turned slippers . . . He had on a long brown linen duster, which was very loose, and evidently intended to wear over another coat in traveling . . . Mr. Lincoln asked me to take a seat in a chair very near a large round table. He took a seat diagonally opposite, the chairs not being over six or seven feet apart . . . In a minute or two, up went one of his long legs onto that table. In a short time up went the other, both being within two and a half feet of my face. I saw several times the front portion of his legs above the ankle. His shirt bosom was open; the attached collar not being buttoned. He several times placed one hand into that open shirt front and waved it a trifle to get the heat out. I now tell you that the front of his legs were [sic] covered with long dark hair, and his breast thickly covered with longer hair. This denotes great strength in man. His hands were very long, the backs of which, and the forearm, were well shaded with hair.

　　As contemporary evidence this is important. How, shortly before his first inauguration, Mr. Lincoln surrendered to a "filamentous outgrowth of the epidermis," and cultivated a beard is usually attributed to the importunities of Grace Bedell, subsequently Grace Bedell Billings, and some *True Republicans,* in New York (cf. *The Lincoln Papers,* I, p. 291), but they were powerfully supported by fashion. Mr. Charles Dickens, a popular English writer, had contributed an article on the subject ("Why Shave?") to a weekly publication, *Household Words,* for August 13, 1853, in the course of which he remarked:

I am no friend to gentlemen who wilfully affect external oddity, while they are within all dull and commonplace. I am not disposed by carrying a beard myself to beard public opinion. But opinions may change; we were not always a nation of shavers. The day may again come when " 'Twill be merry in the hall, when beards wag all," and Britons shall no more be slaves to razors . . . As years multiply and judgment ripens the beard grows, and with it grows, or ought to grow, every man's title to self respect . . . If we could introduce now a reform, we, that have been inured to shaving, may develop very good black beards, most serviceable for all working purposes and a great improvement on bald chins; but the true beauty of the beard remains to be developed . . .

The reform from that very instant gained adherents. Alexander Rowland, in his authoritative monograph, *The Human Hair, Popularly and Physiologically Considered,* London: Piper Brothers & Co., 1853, devoted the tenth chapter (pp. 91-109) to "A Plea for the Beard and Moustache." It is one of the most moving arguments in literature. Dr. G. Calvert Holland, in his *The Constitution of the Animal Creation,* London: John Churchill, 1857, commented (p. 179) on "the remarkable difference in the growth of hair in man and quadrupeds, the cause of which will be found to arise from, and to be in accordance with, the circulation of the blood, and the distribution of nervous power, peculiar to each." Inevitably the movement spread to America. It became part of the Nineteenth Century aesthetic. Bella C. Perry, who was the author of a standard *Treatise on the Human Hair,* published in New Bedford in 1859, concluded his work (pp. 190-192) with "a description of the color and texture of the hair which covered the heads of the Chief Magistrates of this country." According to Dr. Perry, "James Buchanan's is rather inclined to coarseness, perfectly straight, and about as white as that kind of hair usually becomes with one of his age." It was, of course, necessary for Mr. Lincoln, for reasons of state, to be as unlike his predecessor as humanly possible. Like Mr. Buchanan, Mr. Lincoln had what he called "coarse" hair, but his was black. The retiring James was smooth-shaven; in order to emphasize their dissimilarity, accommodate the vogue, please a little girl, and ingratiate himself with the faithful, Father Abraham tossed away his mug, brush, and Damascene blade. It seemed to work.

But about the matter Mr. Lincoln had on his mind: the Library of Congress has recently received a letter which he wrote September 13, 1860. The following passage is to the point:

> The original of the picture you enclose, and which I return was taken from life, and *is,* I think, a very true one, though my wife, and many others, do not—My impression is that their objection arises from the disordered condition of the hair. My judgment is worth nothing in these matters.

The photograph to which he refers (Meserve No. 6) was taken by Alexander Hesler in Chicago, in February, 1857, and was frequently printed during the debates with

Senator Douglas. Looking at it, it is easy to understand Mary Lincoln's embarrassment. His hair *is* a mess. It seems to be all cowlick and quite without elegance. He should have done something about it. It is true that the well-known product of R. B. Semler was not available to him and almost certainly he had, once he was elected to office, no time for a 60-second work out (Bristol-Myers), but there were some acceptable pomades on the market. Research discloses such names as Alpine Hair Balm, Mrs. Sullivan's Preparation, Roche's Inimitable, Bogle's Hyperion Fluid, Delight's Spanish Lustral, Dr. Boylston's Compound, and Lyon's Kathairon. Many of these could be made in the home. Formulae abounded. In some, the principal ingredient was lard, in others it was castor oil, in others still it was mutton suet or beef marrow. These were ordinarily perfumed with essential oils or fresh flowers.

No, there was no excuse for Mr. Lincoln. He was simply a harum-scarum; not all of his remains were suitably interred. It is necessary, therefore, to pursue their posthumous adventures.

The impeccable John Hay was a discriminating, fastidious and sensitive collector of Lincolniana, an avocation which he did not abandon even after history, in the generous form of William McKinley, had imposed upon his suavity the duties of foreign minister. To what extent he was permitted to indulge his passion in those later days is unknown, at least to me, but it *is* clear from his papers that panderers and fellow-members of the guild were privy to it.

Thus, for example, the irrepressible James Grant Wilson wrote to him on November 6, 1902, inquiring:

Do you know of anyone having some of Lincoln's hair? His
son wrote me last week, that he knew of none. I have small
locks of Washington's and Grant's and desired some of Lincoln's, with a view to combining them in a memorial ring to
be deposited hereafter in our museum.

No doubt the idea appealed to Secretary Hay, who must
have blushed in confessing that he had none of the cranial
sprouts of his former master. Perhaps he remembered
the solid gold ring, fashioned by a Scottish jeweler, its
intaglio of white stone incised to represent the bust of
General Washington, and opening on a hinge where, under glass, was a rosewood fragment, carved in the shape
of a coffin, which had come from the casket in which, for
some years, the General's remains had rested. Imbedded
on the splinter were thirteen tiny gold stars. A Mr. Currie
had presented this morbid curiosity to President Lincoln,
who was reported to have said, "I have never worn a ring
before but I shall wear this." Certainly the idea did
not abash John Hay. For as early as February 19, 1893,
he had written to Dr. Charles Sabin Taft:

In the current number of the *Century* you speak of having
a lock of hair from the head of President Lincoln. If you
would care to trade it, I will give you in exchange some hair
from the head of Washington, with a very brief and perfect
pedigree. They were given by Washington to Mrs. Alexander
Hamilton, and her son gave them to me. I make this offer, as
I suppose that nothing less precious would tempt you. If you
would prefer any other consideration, I will give you *anything*
in my *power*.

Presumably the good doctor declined, for twelve years
later, on February 9, 1905, his son, Charles C. Taft, man-

ager of the clothing department in New York's White-
house, addressed the "Hon. John Hayes," from the Arlington Hotel:

I have just arrived in washington this morning from New
York where my family have been residing since 1876.

My Mother Mrs. Dr. Charles Sabin Taft died on the 3d of
the present month. In looking over her papers I came across a
letter from you . . . asking my Father Dr. Charles Sabin
Taft for a lock of Ex President Lincon's hair, and that you
were anxious to purchase it. I have the hair in my possession
now and a cuff button taken from Lincons shirt by my Father
Asst Surgen C. S. Taft at Fords Theatre in the box where he
was assaninated [*sic*] on April 14" 1865.

My Father and Mother while living would never part with
the relics of Lincon, but as I have been put to considerable
expense by the illness and death of my Mother and having a
large family of my own, I am compeled to part with them.

I have a certificate written in my Father's handwriting
certifying to the button his papers and proff that I am his son.
I also enclose a copy of your letter of which I have the
orriginal.

By kindly granting me an interview I can satisfy you in
regard to the truth of my statements.

The Secretary of State, who for reasons which will appear was in a hurry, granted an audience to the stricken
haberdasher and closed the deal. On February 27, 1905,
Charles C. Taft wrote again to Mr. Hay:

According to promise, I herewith send you a copy of my
father's notes written at the time of President Abraham Lincoln's assassination at Ford's Opera House. My father, Dr.
Charles Sabin Taft, at the time, was Assistant Surgeon, U.S.A.,
as you are aware. In reading the above mentioned notes, you
will find a true and detailed history of how the lock of hair

from the head of President Lincoln, of which I sold some to you, and the cuff button President Lincoln wore at the time of his assassination, came into my father's possession. You mentioned a Mr. Latimer [Lambert] of Philadelphia, who, you thought, would be interested or who would buy the cuff button or hair. I tried to find Mr. Latimer in Philadelphia but could not locate him. You also mentioned some gentleman residing in Chicago [Gunther?] who is interested in collecting historical relics. If not asking too much would you kindly give me the names and addresses of any gentlemen whom you may know that would be interested.

How many strands of Lincoln's hair Charles C. Taft inherited from his father is a subject for idle speculation but it must have been quite a swatch. But what are we to think of the provenance of the tress which James Grant Wilson treasured? It will be remembered that, in 1902, General Wilson was in hot pursuit of hirsute Lincolniana in order to complete a "combined" ring. However, in an article devoted to his "Recollections of Lincoln," published in *Putnam's Magazine* for February, 1909, General Wilson wrote:

En passant, the writer may perhaps be permitted to mention that he is the fortunate possessor of a precious memorial of the martyr-President and five other great heirs of fame, in a ring which contains the hair of Washington, Hamilton, Napoleon, Wellington, Lincoln and Grant. The first was received from Washington's adopted son, G. W. P. Custis of Arlington, Virginia; the second from Hamilton's widow, when she was ninety-six and he [Wilson?] sixteen; the third from Captain Frederick Lahrbush of the Sixtieth Rifles, who guarded Napoleon at St. Helena, after being at Waterloo; Wellington's hair from his eldest son, the Second Duke; and Grant's and Lincoln's from the Presidents themselves. When the author . . . asked Mr. Lincoln, on his last birthday, for a lock of his hair to add to Washington's and Hamilton's, he said, "Help yourself, Colonel."

Perhaps Mr. Lincoln *had* said something to this effect. General Wilson, at the time, kept a diary and his account of the episode should be reasonably accurate. But it is doubtful (it seems to me) that General Wilson actually acted on the suggestion and proceeded therewith to snip. If he did, he must have lost or misplaced the follicular foliage before he appealed to John Hay thirty-seven years later. It is barely conceivable that General Wilson did not attain the wisps until he acted as intermediary in another transaction.

In 1912, the Lincoln Fellowship of New York published General Wilson's obituary of William Harrison Lambert. In that glowing tribute to a devout collector, General Wilson wrote:

During the last two decades preceding his death on Saturday morning, June 1, 1912, I occasionally had an opportunity of adding some acceptable Lincoln items to his large collection, but the greatest service of this character in his judgment [*i.e.,* in the judgment of Major Lambert] was acquiring for him, at a cost of six hundred dollars, the large blood-stained lock of hair cut from the President's head when the surgeon was examining the wound made by the assassin's bullet. It was given to Dr. Taft, an army surgeon, among the first to reach the victim, and who was assisting the chief surgeon in charge. Taft's son offered the precious relic to me, and I secured it for the Major, who deemed it his most precious Lincoln treasure, for locks of his hair are more difficult to obtain than those of Washington. It is preserved in a handsome substantial gold box, with an appropriate inscription.

Six hundred dollars! Ah, how the market flourished in those days! Might not William Fleurville, Mr. Lincoln's "Billy the Barber," have amassed a tidy fortune had he only had the foresight to save the sweepings from his floor! But one wonders why, as General Wilson asserts, they were in such short supply.

In that connection allow me to quote from Dr. Taft's account of what transpired at the post-mortem examination:

Mrs. Lincoln [wrote Dr. Taft] sent in a messenger with a request for a lock of hair. Dr. Stone clipped one from the region of the wound, and sent it to her. I extended my hand to him in mute appeal, and received a lock stained with blood, and other surgeons present also received one.

From this I can only conclude that poor Mr. Lincoln's head was ghoulishly if painlessly scalped. There is, moreover, evidence that Major Lambert had been had, for when his lock of Lincoln's hair, enclosed in a fourteen-carat case with a beveled glass top, was sold at auction, it brought only $330.

What price John Hay paid for his part of the Taft legacy is unknown, but he, too, was probably overcharged for the reason that he was, as I have said, in a hurry. He had made his purchase on February 9, 1905; on March 3 he wrote:

DEAR THEODORE:
The hair in this ring is from the head of President Lincoln. Dr. Taft cut it off the night of the assassination and I got it from his son—a brief pedigree.
Please wear it tomorrow; you are one of the men who most thoroughly understand and appreciate Lincoln.

I have had your monogram and Lincoln's engraved on the ring.

Longas, O uitinam[sic], bone dux, ferias Praestes Hesperiae
Yours affectionately
JOHN HAY

And on the same day the gentleman in the White House sent acknowledgment to his "Dear John":

Surely no other President, on the eve of his inauguration, had ever received such a gift from such a friend. I am wearing the ring now; I shall think of it and you as I take the oath tomorrow.

I wonder if you have any idea what your strength and wisdom and sympathy, what the guidance you have given me and the mere delight in your companionship, have meant to me in these three and a half years.

With love and gratitude,
Ever yours
THEODORE ROOSEVELT

The gift was a resounding success. The *Washington Post* announced somewhat carelessly:

On the third finger of President Roosevelt's left hand during the inaugural ceremonies was a heavily embossed gold seal ring. The ring was a present to Mr. Roosevelt yesterday morning from Secretary of State John Hay. Instead of a seal, on the oval flat surface of the ring is a receptacle with a glass face. Under the glass is a lock of hair cut from the head of Abraham Lincoln just after his assassination, and before his death [*sic*].

While in his room and waiting for the ceremonies in the Senate chamber to begin, President Roosevelt called attention to the ring. Secretary Hay, he said, had given it to him, with the expressed wish that it should be worn during his inauguration.

"I am very happy to wear it," added the President, "and shall always value it very highly."

The ring is very like in pattern the one which Mr. Roosevelt wears on the little finger of same hand.

In his *Autobiography,* T. R. recalled his pleasure in the ring, writing:

John Hay was one of the most delightful of companions, one of the most charming of all men of cultivation and action. Our views on foreign affairs coincided absolutely; but, as was natural enough, in domestic matters he felt much more conservative than he did in the days when as a young man he was private secretary to the great radical democratic leader of the '60's, Abraham Lincoln. . . . When I was inaugurated on March 4, 1905, I wore a ring he sent me the evening before, containing the hair of Abraham Lincoln. This ring was on my finger when the Chief Justice administered to me the oath of allegiance to the United States; I often thereafter told John Hay that when I wore such a ring on such an occasion I bound myself more than ever to treat the Constitution, after the manner of Abraham Lincoln, as a document which put human rights above property rights when the two conflicted.

Hay the giver and Roosevelt the given are, as the saying goes, no more; but the hair, in its surrounding of splendor, is understood to survive at Sagamore Hill.

Lincoln and the Image
of America

Addressed to the Lincoln Fellowship of Hamilton,
Ontario

ANYONE in my position must ask himself what he is doing here. For a trespasser to be permitted to cross a border
and there to expatiate upon his favorite theme is an act
of forbearance and charity far beyond the reasonable expectations of a generous race. But when such an intrusion
for such an object is openly and cordially invited, the circumstance shatters the barriers of incredibility.

The present instance is the more extraordinary because
of the heavy obligation which Mr. Lincoln's reputation
owes to the work of his British partisans. That noble
lord, Godfrey Charnwood, gave to the last generation the
most satisfactory synthesis of Lincoln's life; Colin Bal-
lard, C.B., C.M.G., discovered Lincoln's military genius;
John Drinkwater first successfully exhibited the dramatic
content and conflict of the Lincoln story; Raymond Mas-
sey, of this Province, transmitted to our eyes and ears an
enduring impersonation of a rising Illinoisan. By some
kind of tribal instinct they have set a standard of excel-

lence difficult for Mr. Lincoln's countrymen comfortably to attain. It is sheer presumption, therefore, for an upstart to discuss a subject which you understand so much more easily, so much more clearly, so much more intuitively, so much more dispassionately than ever I will understand it.

So situated I can excuse myself only by appeal to common interest and comparable experience.

These are, for both of us, days of ceremonial. We pass through the precedent, protocol and propriety period. You crown a gracious Sovereign; we induct a Chief Magistrate. Her Majesty and His Excellency are not unacquainted. In contrast how paralyzed with prematurity was the autumn of 1860. The Prince of Wales came to Hamilton, in mid-September, attended a philharmonic concert, visited the public schools, held a levée at the Royal Hotel, had a look at the agricultural exhibition, was honored with a "very grand ball" at the Anglo-American, dedicated the water works, and thereafter proceeded to our Middle West.

On September 26, he passed through Springfield, then enjoying some notoriety as the residence of a candidate for the Presidency of the United States. A member of the Prince's entourage saw the candidate's home and reported that it was "very small and plain." But unhappily for history, the two heirs apparent did not meet. Abraham Lincoln later informed a correspondent of the *New York Herald* that "had he not occupied his peculiar position, so that he could have joined his fellow citizens in common in a welcome to the representative of the British government without having his motive misrepresented and a charge of immodesty brought against him, he would have taken measures to notice properly the passage of the Prince." Mr. Lincoln added, "Being thus situated, and not able to take any lead in the matter, I remained here at the State House, where I met so many sovereigns during the day that really the Prince had come and gone before I knew it." The *Herald's* man understood that "the Prince expressed a desire to see Mr. Lincoln, learning that he was likely to be the next President . . . ; but the fact was not early enough known to effect the arrangements."

But it should not be supposed that royalty had left no impress upon the townsmen of the capital of Illinois. Actually, it made quite a stir and it was not many days before this record appeared in a Springfield paper: "Among the passing events of the week, none proved more interesting than a sight of the young Prince of Wales, yet he did not create any more sensation than does the magnificent Clothing manufactured by Hammerslough & Brothers, which received the first premium at the late State Fair at Jacksonville."

Nor is it accurate to assume that Abraham Lincoln was as indifferent as he pretended. After he was installed in the White House, he wrote to the Victorian mother: "Accidents, . . . incidental to all States, and passions, common to all nations, often tend to disturb the harmony so necessary and so proper between the two countries, and to convert them into enemies. It was reserved for Your Majesty in sending your son, the Heir Apparent of the British Throne, on a visit among us, to inaugurate a policy destined to counteract these injurious tendencies."

To be sure there were episodes in the course of Mr. Lincoln's administration which gave rise to international tensions; there were recommendations to fortify the boundary and to float a navy on the Lakes; but for Mr. Lincoln personally and for his cause it is unlikely that there existed any widespread sentiment of ill will on the part of the Canadians. When their Finance Minister came to Washington, late in 1861, he wrote his wife that he had seen the President and had had a long and satisfactory interview with him. "He is," Alexander Galt explained, "very tall, thin, and with marked features, appears fond of anecdote, of which he has a fund. I liked him for his straightforward, strong commonsense." His compatriots shared Sir Alexander's view.

That they, too, liked him; that they were sensitive to his greatness, and aware of his glowing spirit, was publicly proclaimed within the fortnight following his outrageous murder, when E. S. Leavenworth's Book and Job Office, of St. Catharines, published a pamphlet of thirty-nine pages, entitled *Maple Leaves from Canada, For the Grave of Abraham Lincoln.*

Now, nearly a century later, that slender brochure is one of the most highly prized and eagerly sought contributions to the vast literature of Lincolniana. Recently a prominent collector informed me that he had tried for fifteen years to procure a copy, but so far without success.

It begins with the Rev. Mr. Robert Norton's memorial discourse and contains these moving lines:

God loves America and tens of thousands of his saints have dwelt, and sighed, and prayed, among the people, whose national crimes they knew not how to remove. . . . A wail of horror thrills across the American continent. Slavery and Abraham Lincoln have died together. The one shall be hurled into the pit of everlasting execration—the name of the other shall ring in the songs and thanksgivings of a redeemed people for evermore. . . . In his private life, as I learn from one who knew him well in his Illinois home, he was plain, frank and affable, and the law of kindness was on his lips.

The Norton sermon is followed by an address delivered by the Rev. Dr. Robert Ferrier Burns, and contains the following passage:

As the alienated brothers in the days of old, met beside the grave of their father Abraham, so, over the honored remains of Abraham Lincoln will these two peoples [the people of Canada and the people of the United States] shake hands, and in his grave bury for ever every ground of variance. . . . Yes we be brethren—having the same origin and destiny. One in laws, one in language, one in faith, one in the great fundamentals of national character . . . History will give to this remarkable man a higher niche than will be assigned to him now. We are too near him to judge righteous judgment. A century hence his name will be more fragrant. The difficulties of his position will be more fully appreciated. The asperities awakened by the present war will be forgotten. Then yet more luminously will Abraham Lincoln shine forth a bright and beautiful illustration of whatsoever things are true, honest, lovely and of good report—a stimulus and a study to the rising generations—a model for our coming men.

Maple Leaves concludes with an account of a public meeting, held in Fowler's Hall, on April 20, 1865. Among the speakers, on that occasion, was the Honorable J. G. Currie, M.L.C., who remarked that "in thus giving utterance to our sympathy, he believed we only anticipated a similar expression of condolence from our beloved Queen. He had no doubt that of all the addresses of condolence which the widow of the late President would receive, "none will be kinder or more affectionate than the autograph letter of our gracious Sovereign."

Councilor Currie must have possessed telepathic powers, for exactly one week later, Professor Goldwin Smith wrote from Oxford to Dr. A. P. Stanley, Dean of Westminster:

The murder of the President, who was the ministry not only of clemency at home but of moderation abroad, so greatly increases the danger to the peace of the world from that quarter, that I feel it almost a duty to let you know how much good might be done, and how much evil might be averted, by a *personal* expression of sympathy from the Queen.

Towards her personally, the affection of the American people, displayed in the passionate enthusiasm with which they received her son, has never abated, in spite of all the bitterness between the two nations. It springs from the deepest part of their character, and survives all political estrangement. She cannot be a greater object of household love and veneration in her own dominions than she is throughout the Northern States.

The words of a Prime Minister will be civilly acknowledged by the authorities and the Press; they will have no effect on the heart of the people.

Professor Smith had confirmed the assurances which Abraham Lincoln once had sent to the Working-Men of Manchester: "Your Queen," Mr. Lincoln had written, "is respected and esteemed in your own country only more than she is by the kindred nation which has its home on this side of the Atlantic."

Dean Stanley was impressed by the note of urgency; he transmitted Professor Smith's letter to Her Majesty.

Through a strange coincidence Lord John Russell had written her in similar vein. The Queen was persuaded by the opportunity. Within forty-eight hours she had composed and dispatched this message:

Dear Madam,
   Though a Stranger to you I cannot remain silent when so terrible a Calamity has fallen upon you & your Country & must personally express my *deep* & *heartfelt* sympathy with you under the shocking circumstances of your present dreadful misfortune.
   No one can better appreciate than *I* can, who am myself *utterly broken hearted* by the loss of my own beloved husband, who was the *Light* of my Life—my Stay—my ALL,— what your sufferings must be; and I earnestly pray that you may be supported by Him to whom Alone the sorely stricken can look for comfort in this hour of heavy affliction.

On the following Monday, Earl Russell told the House of Lords that "Her Majesty has . . . been pleased to write a private letter to Mrs. Lincoln, expressive of sympathy with that lady in her great and sudden bereavement." According to a statement in *The Times,* the announcement was received with "cheers."

In due course the message reached the widow Lincoln. But the British people who must confidently have expected that it would be promptly released, transcribed, and widely distributed in the public prints would be in for a long wait. Irony intervened. The Queen's advisers had not counted on the penetration of Victorianism among the Yankees. Her subjects were mystified; one of them, in 1867, asked Abraham Lincoln's son if it was true that the Queen had written to his mother. Robert Lincoln answered: "Yes, a long letter of four pages. We have been often urged to publish it, but we have decided not to do so, as it was evidently written with no idea of publicity, though it would be greatly to the honor of the Queen if it were made known; but it was so evidently the unrestrained outpouring of sympathy from a full heart, that we felt it would be a violation of propriety to publish it, at least during the lifetime of the writer."

The Lincolns held fast to that decision. It was unaltered when Robert Lincoln became Minister to Victoria's court. It was unaltered when he died in 1926, but shortly thereafter his widow presented it to the Library of Congress. There it has been frequently exhibited; there at last it has achieved the intention for which it was written; there it has, as Goldwin Smith knew it would, affected "the heart of the people." And not the American people only, but others as well. Ten years ago, a charming lady, garbed all in green, stood before its case, and with unfeigned interest read every word. Her name is Elizabeth. She directed the attention of Philip, her husband, to that bold, round hand; the crowded, emphatic, dolorous underscoring; the cry of understanding and its pathos. A wonderfully faithful reproduction of the Queen's letter was recently carried to Buckingham Palace.

But if anyone in my position must ask himself what he is doing here, let him remind himself that the Lincoln Fellowship, of Hamilton, continues an Ontario tradition which began so long ago with *Maple Leaves*. For if it was proper to pay tribute to him when he died, to close places of business for the hour of his funeral, and to hold memorial services in his honor, so it is fitting that his birthday should be observed. Dr. Burns was right: Canadians and Americans are "one . . . in the great fundamental elements of national character." And Abraham Lincoln was one of us; he was consciously a North American. The evidence is in his speeches at Cincinnati in 1859 and 1861; it is in his address on the fallen at the field of Gettysburg in 1863. Like his new nation, Abraham Lincoln was brought forth on this continent. He was the product of a new time in a new world.

Mr. Lincoln said of his political idol, Henry Clay, that "the spell—the long enduring spell—with which the souls of men were bound to him, is a miracle." We may apply his words to Mr. Lincoln himself. But I can neither explain the miracle nor solve the mystery. The proof of his hold upon the minds and hearts of men is all around us. But the secret of the hold is still his own. Those who seek the answers become only more confounded. The excesses of adulation which have been uttered in his praise are only less fallacious than the attempts to reduce him to the level of common clay.

In the summer of 1856, he told a large audience at Kalamazoo:

We are a great empire. We are eighty years old. We stand at once the wonder and admiration of the whole world, and we must enquire what it is that has given us so much prosperity. This cause is that every man can make himself.

Other men have made themselves but they have not made another Lincoln. Before and after him were those, born in log cabins in the wilderness, who ultimately became tenants of the White House, but none who in a later day exercises so benign an influence. No, the Lincoln story is more than a "success story" as related by Oliver Optic, or Horatio Alger, or Ralph Henry Barbour, or the hacks of the *American Magazine*. Lincoln was a Western David, come from the land, to slay, in debate, a "little giant," to govern with his people, and to write the psalms of democracy. In some strange, some unique way, he was compounded of those virtues which his fellows most passionately approve and those faults which his fellows most cheerfully condone.

His rude appearance shocked the exquisite sensibilities of his refined associates. He cut a clumsy, grotesque figure on a horse. He received distinguished foreigners before brushing his hair and allowed them a glimpse of his long coarse stockings. When he insisted upon telling a story, a feeling of restless uneasiness swept over his ministers— it might be, it often was, earthy and inelegant. He could be frivolous at sober moments. A politician all his life, the less edifying aspects of politics did not always shock him. He was complicated, inhibited, extroverted, many-sided, frequently inscrutable and exasperating. He was obstinate and self-reliant and resistant to expediency and emotional and sentimental.

But his virtues were so towering that they shaded the deficiencies they could not quite destroy. In a memorandum, he once noted: "I claim no extraordinary exemption from personal ambition. That I like preferment as well as the average of men may be admitted." But when, a few months before his nomination for the Presidency, he wrote an outline of his life, he confessed: "there isn't much of it because there isn't much of me." To a judge who asked permission to dedicate to him a work on international law, Mr. Lincoln replied: "Gratefully accepting the proffered honor, I give the leave, begging only that the inscription may be in modest terms, not representing me as a man of great learning, or a very extraordinary one in any respect." On his way to his first inauguration, he told the members of the New York Legislature: "It is true that while I hold myself, without mock modesty, the humblest of all individuals that have ever been elevated to the Presidency, I have a more difficult task to perform than any one of them."

He never learned to spell and in his private correspondence he could split an infinitive as thoroughly as he could split a rail. To a confidant he confessed: "With educated people, I suppose, punctuation is a matter of rule; with me it is a matter of feeling. But I must say that I have a great respect for the semi-colon; it's a very useful little chap." When a chance acquaintance congratulated him upon the clarity and conviction of his address at New York's Cooper Institute, Mr. Lincoln reminisced:

I remember how, when a mere child, I used to get irritated when anybody talked to me in a way I could not understand. I don't think I ever got angry at anything else in my life. But that always disturbed my temper, and has ever since. I remember going to my little bedroom, after hearing the neighbors talk of an evening with my father, and spending no small part of the night walking up and down, and trying to make out what was the exact meaning of some of their, to me, dark sayings. I could not sleep, though I often tried to, when I got on such a hunt after an idea, until I had caught it; and when I thought I had got it, I was not satisfied until I had repeated it over and over, until I had put it in language plain enough, as I thought, for any boy I knew to comprehend.

He understood the importance of popularity to a cause. "In this age, and this country," he wrote, "public sentiment is every thing. *With* it, nothing can fail; *against* it, nothing can succeed. Whoever molds public sentiment, goes deeper than he who enacts statutes, or pronounces judicial decisions."

He made mistakes and was the first to discover and proclaim them. He had the happy faculty of laughing at himself. He assumed the highest office in the land without the slightest previous administrative experience of any kind, but incomparably conducted the Union through its most harrowing crisis. He was not a conspicuously good judge of men; he was repeatedly disillusioned; but he was never cynical; he never lost confidence in those he served. After his election, when Southern anger threatened the entity of the Republic, he told a gathering in Bloomington:

I think very much of the people, as an old friend said he thought of woman. He said when he lost his first wife, who had been a great help to him in his business, he thought he was ruined—that he could never find another to fill her place. At length, however, he married another, who he found did quite as well as the first, and that his opinion now was that any woman would do well who was well done by. So I think of the whole people of this nation—they will ever do well if well done by. We will try to do well by them in all parts of the country, North and South, with entire confidence that all will be well with all of us.

Perhaps we would understand Mr. Lincoln better, if his friends had not been so eager to tell us exactly what kind of a man he really was. His friends have misled us, not deliberately perhaps, but because vanity imposed a fraudulent impression that when they were not his peers they were his superiors. Certainly his old law partner, William Henry Herndon labored under this delusion.

In his lectures on, and his biography of, Mr. Lincoln, Herndon reported how he [Herndon] had visited Niagara Falls in the summer of 1858. A few days after his return to Springfield, Herndon gave Mr. Lincoln an excited account of the wonder he had seen. These are Herndon's words:

As I warmed up with the subject my descriptive powers expanded accordingly. The mad rush of water, the roar, the rapids, and the rainbow furnished me with an abundance of material for a stirring and impressive picture. The recollection of the gigantic and awe-inspiring scene stimulated my exuberant powers to the highest pitch. After well-nigh exhausting myself in the effort I turned to Lincoln for his opinion. "What," I inquired, "made the deepest impression on you when you stood in the presence of this great natural wonder?" I shall never forget his answer, because it in a very characteristic way illustrates how he looked at everything. "The thing that struck me most forcibly when I saw the Falls," he responded, "was, where in the world did all that water come from?" He had no eye for the magnificence and grandeur of the scene, for the rapids, the mist, the angry waters, and the roar of the whirlpool, but his mind working in its accustomed channel, heedless of beauty or awe, followed irresistibly back to the first cause. It was in this light he viewed every question. However great the verbal foliage that concealed the nakedness of a good idea Lincoln stripped it all down till he could see clear the way between cause and effect.

That was Billy Herndon's estimate, diagnosis and final verdict, but Billy was wrong as only a self-inflated cockalorum can be. For in the Manuscripts Division of the Library of Congress is an unfinished essay. These are passages from it:

Niagara Falls! By what mysterious power is it that millions and millions, are drawn from all parts of the world to gaze upon Niagara Falls. Every effect is just such as any inteligent [*sic*] man knowing the causes, would anticipate, without [seeing] it. If the water moving onward in a great river, reaches a point where there is a perpendicular jog, of a hundred feet in descent, in the bottom of the river,—it is plain that the water will have a violent and continuous plunge at this point. It is also plain the water, thus plunging, will foam, and roar, and send up a mist continuously, in which last, during sunshine, there will be perpetual rain-bows. The mere physical of Niagara Falls is only this. . . . But still there is more. It calls up the indefinite past. When Columbus first sought this continent—when Christ suffered on the cross—when Moses led Israel through the Red Sea—nay, even when Adam first came from the hand of his Maker—then as now, Niagara was roaring here. The eyes of that species of extinct giants, whose bones fill the mounds of America, have gazed on Niagara, as ours do now. Co[n]temporary with the whole race of men, and older than the first man, Niagara is strong and fresh today as ten thousand years ago. The Mammoth and Mastadon—now so long dead, that fragments of their monstrous bones, alone testify, that they ever lived, have gazed on Niagara. In that long—long time, never still for a single moment. Never dried, never frozen, never slept, never rested.

Here, the Emersonian effusion breaks off. It is written in the hand of one whom Billy Herndon insisted was denied a sense of "the Grand and Sublime":—Abraham Lincoln. As to the circumstances under which it was written, there is no clue. Mr. Lincoln first saw Niagara in the fall of 1848. With Mrs. Lincoln he visited the Canadian side of the Falls in July, 1857, returning to Springfield by way of Toronto. It is not inconceivable that it is a draft of a sentiment inscribed in one of those albums or "public books" where pilgrims were urged to record their feelings after a sight of the magnificent work of nature. In that event, the fair copy may survive somewhere in this neighborhood.

But there is physical evidence that Mr. Lincoln set some store by it, for stains on the leaves attest that it was once in that shabby, black bag, soaked in Cleveland's snow, and containing his inaugural and a few other precious papers which Mr. Lincoln brought on his circuitous journey to Washington in February, 1861. Long before he left Springfield his itinerary had been fixed. But late in January, Thomas Reynolds had written him from "Hamilton, Canada West":

Permit me to express the hope that in making arrangements for your progress to Washington, you will select the Great Western route.

In the event of your doing so allow me on behalf of this Company, to assure you, that every effort shall be made to ensure your comfort & that of your friends accompanying you.

It will afford me much pleasure to appropriate to your exclusive use one of our most commodious passenger cars, and in every way in my power to contribute to the comfort of your journey from Detroit to Suspension Bridge, our Eastern Terminus.

Mr. Lincoln was already committed to go by another way. But he gave terse instructions to his secretary: "Answer this respectfully." Perhaps he thought some last-minute change of plans might permit him to return to Table Rock. Or perhaps he thought of his apostrophe to Niagara as an illustration for a speech to be delivered at some station where the train would rumble to a stop. Perhaps he would refer to Niagara's rushes as the spirit of man that would never be contained. Perhaps in the whirlpool he would find symbol of a long struggle. Perhaps the rainbow was, to him, the promise of "the last, best, hope of earth." For this much is certain: Lincoln's image of America was an environment of freedom.

He expressed it in his war message to Congress on July 4, 1861:

This is essentially a people's contest—On the side of the Union, it is a struggle for maintaining in the world that form, and substance of government, whose leading object is to elevate the condition of men—to lift artificial weights from all shoulders—to clear the paths of laudable pursuit for all— to afford all an unfettered start and a fair chance in the race of life.

He expressed it again, three years later, in addressing a regiment of Ohio soldiers:

It is not merely for to-day, but for all time to come that we should perpetuate for our children's children this great and free government, which we have enjoyed all our lives. I beg you to remember this, not merely for my sake, but for yours. I happen temporarily to occupy this big White House. I am a living witness that any one of your children may look to come here as my father's child has. It is in order that each of you may have through this free government . . . an open field and a fair chance for your industry, enterprise and intelligence; that you may all have equal privileges in the race of life, with all its desirable human aspirations. It is for this the struggle should be maintained, that we may not lose our birthright.

And even in the darkest days of war this man, this Lincoln could exclaim:

Thanks to all. For the great Republic—for the principle it lives by, and keeps alive—for man's vast future, thanks to all.

And perhaps, upon his birthday, Canadians will join me in offering thanks for him.

Great Day in "Ottaway"

THE DEBATES BEGIN
DOUGLAS AND LINCOLN FACE TO FACE

Special to the Washington Post and Times Herald
Ottawa, Ills., August 21, 1858.

BEFORE a vast multitude, the first of the widely adver-
tised "joint discussions," between Abraham Lincoln, Republican candidate for United States Senator, and his
Democratic rival, the incumbent, Stephen Arnold Douglas, took place in this thriving town this afternoon. Surely
if the pace, pitch and passion aroused to-day can be sustained, this will prove to be the most exciting canvass in
our political history.

The Scene

The contestants are no strangers to this place. Both
have visited "Ottaway" many times and for each it evokes
memories. It was, for example, here at the confluence of
the Fox and the Illinois, that young Indian fighter Abraham Lincoln was, in the Spring of 1832, mustered out of
one company and into another by a Lieutenant Robert
Anderson. Again, in June of 1851, lawyer Douglas represented the plaintiff and lawyer Lincoln the defendant in
the case of Dunlap *v.* Smith *et al.* Less than two years ago,
that "new" Republican, Mr. Lincoln, made a speech in

behalf of "Pathfinder" Fremont's unsuccessful candidacy for the Presidency from this same park. But never before have the presence of Judge Douglas, the nationally renowned statesman, and Abraham Lincoln, a prairie politician almost unknown beyond the boundaries of the State, attracted so much and such wide attention to Ottawa.

To-day, for the first time, shorthand reporters have recorded a political debate. The stenographers respectively represent the Chicago *Times* (Democratic) and the Chicago *Press and Tribune* (Republican). But correspondents from the Metropolitan dailies of the East are also here to cover the proceedings. To one of them, John W. Forney, of the Philadelphia *Press,* Judge Douglas, a day or two since, confided a high opinion of his adversary, saying: "I shall have my hands full. He [Lincoln] is the strong man of his party—full of wit, facts, dates, and the best stump-speaker with his droll way and dry jokes, in the West. He is as honest as he is shrewd; and if I can beat him, my victory will be hardly won."

From daylight this morning until three o'clock this afternoon this beleaguered town was deluged with dust from the dirt roads which, mingled as it was with the intense rays of the sun, produced a heavy haze. Before breakfast the invading hosts began to enter the city from all directions. By wagon, carriage, buggy, by horseback and afoot, by train and boat they came. Ottawa, in holiday mood, was ready for them. Bunting decorated buildings. Flags, ensigns and devices were everywhere. Soon two brass twelve pounders were banging away. Military companies were marching. Bands played popular airs and to their din was added the percussion and the shrill of fife and drum corps. Peddlers behind their stands hawked Lincoln badges or Douglas badges according to their choice. Marshals and their aides, identified by gaudy sashes, rode furiously and importantly about. Politicians were canvassing and quarreling on every corner. There was an occasional resort to physical violence. Bars were crowded. But, on the whole, the crowd was good-natured and eager with expectancy.

The Democrats had declined to accept the suggestion of a joint reception for the speakers. In consequence, at eleven o'clock, two long processions formed, one, with William H. L. Wallace at its head, proceeded to the depot of the Rock Island Railroad; the other made its way to Buffalo Rock, a place about four miles from town. At a little after noon, the special train, of seventeen cars, from Chicago steamed in bearing Abraham Lincoln who had boarded it at Morris. At his appearance a mighty cheer arose.

He was wearing a frock-coat, waistcoat and trousers of black alpaca; a white shirt; a narrow black bow tie; a pair of new Lynn pegged boots; and, on his head, a battered silk hat, now several sizes too large by reason of his habit of stuffing the crown with important papers. In his hands he carried an umbrella and a well-worn carpetbag.

Behind him came Henry Clay Whitney, the Chicago lawyer who, while cheers continued and noisy greetings were exchanged, told this reporter: "He sat with me throughout the journey; and I am thus enabled to know for myself that this remarkable man exhibits not the slightest trace of excitement or nervousness at the threshold of one of the fiercest political contests in this or in any other country. We talked about matters other than the impending debate. I merely alluded to that as we neared here to which he calmly and indifferently replied that he is ready."

Mr. Lincoln was placed in a carriage beautifully decorated with evergreens and mottoes by the young ladies of Ottawa. With bands playing, the procession reformed and moved through the enormous throngs who blockaded the streets and sidewalks, roaring their approval of the Republican aspirant. Crossing the bridge there was a salvo of applause from the men and women standing on two large canal boats which have come over from Marseilles and Morris.

Judge Douglas drove over this morning from the city of Peru, about sixteen miles from Ottawa, in an elegant carriage drawn by four splendid horses. With him came a large delegation on horseback and in vehicles. As it passed along the road, the procession was augmented at every crossing and stopping place. At Buffalo Rock it was further increased by the official reception party. On entering Ottawa, a little after twelve, people from the sidewalks, from windows, piazzas, house-tops, and every available standing point cheered and welcomed him, amid the booming of cannon and the strains of martial music.

In the center of town the two processions met briefly but each wended its way by different routes through the principal streets. As Senator Douglas neared the Geiger House on La Salle Street, it was almost impossible for the carriages to force their way through the solid mass of humanity that blocked up the streets, clung to the carriage and sought to grasp the Senator by the hand. The shouts and cheers that arose on his approach were deafening. When at last his carriage halted before the hotel, there arose one spontaneous shout that seemed to rend the very air. Again and again the cheers went up, while the Little Giant stood in the open carriage with head uncovered, gracefully bowing to his tumultuous admirers on every side. As soon as a semblance of order could be restored, he was eloquently welcomed by H. W. H. Cushman, Esq.

Meanwhile, the Lincoln parade, equally triumphant, passed around the square to the residence of Mayor Glover where he is an overnight guest. There he was given another prolonged ovation before his full-throated henchmen temporarily disbanded for dinner.

The ceremonies were scheduled to begin at two o'clock but an hour earlier the crowd in the exposed and un-shaded square had assembled. Ottawa has a population of about six thousand people, but to-day more than twelve thousand wild enthusiasts struggled in the summer heat for vantage points from which to see and hear the champions of the two great parties. The rush and crush were really extraordinary. The speaking stand foolishly had been left unguarded and was so crowded before the officers of the day arrived that half an hour was consumed in a battle to make room for the speakers and reporters. Even then the accommodations were of the most wretched sort. Two or three times the surge of people towards the platform nearly drove the reporters off, and at one point half a dozen clowns on the roof broke through some of the boards and deposited themselves upon the heads of startled members of the Democratic reception committee. There were no casualties.

Lincoln and Douglas sat there waiting for the mass delirium to spend itself. They were an oddly contrasted pair. As Easterners well know, Douglas is a short, thick-set, burly man, standing just over five feet, with a large round head, heavy hair, dark complexion, a polished platform manner, and a rich and sonorous voice. He is used to power and acclaim; there are those who think him arrogant. He looked out upon that boisterous audience with complete assurance and, perhaps, with a trace of defiant contempt.

His rival, Lincoln, is physically and intellectually his opposite. A native of Kentucky, sprung from poor white parents, he is in height six feet four inches and weighs one hundred and eighty pounds. He is slender, angular, awkward. His face is sharp, large-featured, smooth-shaven and quite unprepossessing. His eyes are deep set, under heavy brows; his forehead is high and retreating; his hair dark and stranger to a comb. In repose he is anything but handsome, and yet when animated the fire of genius glows in every feature. Then his eyes sparkle and he becomes a man of rare power and strong magnetic influence. His voice is round enough and carries well but has a tendency to shrillness and, when laboring under excitement, has a squeaky quality. To-day, as he sat there waiting, he was plain, modest and unembarrassed.

It had been agreed that Judge Douglas should open the debate, speaking for one hour; then for an hour and a half Mr. Lincoln should hold the floor; after which Judge Douglas would be allowed half an hour for rejoinder. As to subject, it was known that it would be concentered on the great, national problem which divides this unhappy country: the status of the Negro with particular reference to his status in the Territories and general reference to the doctrine, a favorite of Judge Douglas, of popular sovereignty.

At last the disturbance diminished to a point where Judge Douglas could begin. He spoke of his early acquaintance with his rival. "Lincoln," he said, "is one of those peculiar men who perform with admirable skill everything which they undertake. I made as good a school teacher as I could and when a cabinet maker I made a good bedstead and tables, although my old boss said I succeeded better with bureaus and secretaries than anything else [cheers]; but I believe that Lincoln was always more successful in business than I, for his business enabled him to get into the legislature. I met him there, however, and had a sympathy with him, because of the uphill struggle we both had in life. He was then just as good at telling an anecdote as now. He could beat any of the boys wrestling, or running a foot race, in pitching quoits or tossing a copper, could ruin more liquor than all the boys of the town together [uproarious laughter], and the dignity and impartiality with which he presided at a horse race or fist fight, excited the admiration and won the praise of everybody that was present and participated."

He accused the Republicans of being a combination of deserters from the old Whig and the old Democratic parties bent upon slavery's abolition. He criticized the "House Divided" speech that Lincoln made in Springfield a few weeks ago, complaining: "He [Lincoln] says that it [the country] has existed for about seventy years thus divided, and yet he tells you that it cannot endure permanently on the same principles and in the same relative condition in which our fathers made it." He wanted to know, "Why can it not exist divided into free and slave States?" In his opinion, "uniformity in the local laws and institutions of the different States is neither possible nor desirable."

He wished to be perfectly understood. "For one," he cried, "I am opposed to Negro citizenship in any and every form [cheers]. I believe this country was made on the white basis. I believe it was made by white men, for the benefit of white men and their posterity forever, and I am in favor of confining citizenship to white men, men of European birth and descent, instead of conferring it upon Negroes, Indians and other inferior races." Here there were shouts of "Good for you!" and "Douglas forever."

The Judge scoffed at those who draw false interpretations from our ancient charter and thereby impose upon the credulities and consciences of their fellows. With emphatic gestures, he warned his audience: "Mr. Lincoln, following the example and lead of all the little abolition orators, who go around and lecture in the basements of schools and churches, reads from the Declaration of Independence that all men were created equal, and then asks how can you deprive a Negro of that equality which God and the Declaration of Independence awards to him. He and they maintain that Negro equality is guaranteed by the laws of God, and that it is asserted in the Declaration of Independence. If they think so, of course they have a right to say so, and so vote. I do not question Mr. Lincoln's conscientious belief that the Negro was made his equal, and hence is his brother [laughter], but for my own part, I do not regard the Negro as my equal, and positively deny that he is my brother or any kin to me whatever." Wiping his face with a large handkerchief, the Judge went on: "Now, I do not believe that the Almighty ever intended the Negro to be the equal of the white man. If he did, he has been a long time demonstrating the fact [cheers]. For thousands of years the Negro has been a race upon the earth and during all that time, in all latitudes and climates, wherever he has wandered or been taken, he has been inferior to the race which he has there met. . . . I do not hold that because the Negro is our inferior that therefore he ought to be a slave. By no means can such a conclusion be drawn from what I have said. On the contrary, I hold that humanity and Christianity both require that the Negro shall have and enjoy every right, every privilege, and every immunity consistent with the safety of the society in which he lives." Surely the country has no more outspoken an advocate of segregation than this transplanted New Englander, Stephen Douglas. This afternoon, as usual, he remanded the question of the "peculiar institution" to local jurisdiction, shouting, "I hold that . . . every State of this Union is a sovereign power, with the right to do as it pleases upon this question of slavery, and upon all its domestic institutions." Upon that principle he made his case.

When Mr. Lincoln rose to reply there was a prolonged demonstration, until finally he was obliged to interrupt his noisy adherents a little impatiently: "My fellow citizens don't take up my time." Then he went on to insist that he is not and never has been an integrationist. He put on his spectacles and for seven minutes read, by way of a brief or creed, from a speech delivered at Peoria nearly four years ago. Swinging his body from side to side when wishing to make a point, he declared: "Anything that argues me into his [Douglas's] idea of perfect social and political equality with the Negro, is but a specious and fantastic arrangement of words, by which a man can prove a horse chestnut to be a chestnut horse [laughter]. I will say here, while upon this subject, that I have no purpose directly or indirectly to interfere with the institution of slavery in the States where it exists. I believe I have no lawful right to do so, and I have no inclination to do so. I have no purpose to introduce political and social equality between the white and the black races. There is a physical difference between the two, which in my judgment will forever forbid their living together upon the footing of perfect equality, and inasmuch as it becomes a necessity that there must be a difference, I, as well as Judge Douglas, am in favor of the race to which I belong, having the superior position. I have never said anything to the contrary, but I hold that notwithstanding all this, there is no reason in the world why the Negro is not entitled to all the natural rights enumerated in the Declaration of Independence, the right to life, liberty and the pursuit of happiness [loud cheers]. I hold that he is as much entitled to these as the white man. I agree with Judge Douglas he is not my equal in many respects— certainly not in color, perhaps not in moral or intellectual endowment. But in the right to eat the bread, without leave of anybody else, which his own hand earns, *he is my equal and the equal of Judge Douglas, and the equal of every living man."* This was greeted with a burst of applause.

Mr. Lincoln drew laughter and more applause when he said: "He [Douglas] has read from my speech in Springfield, in which I say that 'a house divided against itself cannot stand.' Does the Judge say it *can stand?* If he does, then there is a question of veracity, not between him and

me, but between the Judge and an Authority of a somewhat higher character."

With respect to the great issue, Mr. Lincoln insisted:
"I leave it to you to say whether, in the history of our
Government, this institution of slavery has not always
failed to be a bond of union, and, on the contrary, been
an apple of discord and an element of division. I ask you
to consider whether, so long as the moral constitution of
men's minds shall continue to be the same, after this generation and assemblage shall sink into the grave, and another race shall arise, with the same moral and intellectual
development we have—whether, if that institution is
standing in the same irritating position it now is, it will
not continue an element of division?" To this rhetorical
question came loud answers, "Yes, yes."

But Mr. Lincoln, who confesses to a hope that slavery
may be on the way to ultimate extinction, is disturbed by
a changed attitude on the part of Douglas and the Judge's
partisans. Mr. Lincoln said: "Lately I think that he, and
those acting with him, have placed that institution on a
new basis, which looks to the *perpetuity and nationalization of slavery.*

As to squatters' rights, Mr. Lincoln commented: "I will
state—and I have an able man to watch me—my understanding is that popular sovereignty, as now applied to the
question of slavery, does allow the people of a territory to
have slavery if they want to, but does not allow them *not*
to have it if they *do not* want it." This was greeted with
laughter and applause.

Mr. Lincoln alluded to a compliment which Judge
Douglas had paid him in a speech at Chicago last month
and went on: "I was a little 'taken' for it came from a

great man. I was not very accustomed to flattery, and it came the sweeter to me. I was rather like the Hoosier, with the gingerbread, when he said he reckoned he loved it better than any other man, and got less of it." This brought down the house.

Lincoln, in turn, paid tribute to his rival's qualities of leadership when he said: "With public sentiment, nothing can fail; without it nothing can succeed. Consequently he who molds public sentiment, goes deeper than he who enacts statutes or pronounces decisions. He makes statutes and decisions possible or impossible to be executed. This must be borne in mind, as also the additional fact that Judge Douglas is a man of vast influence, so great that it is enough for many men to profess to believe anything, when they once find out that Judge Douglas professes to believe it."

Mr. Lincoln's allotted time was running out. He glanced at his watch and wound up with these words: "When he [Douglas] invites any people willing to have slavery, to establish it, he is blowing out the moral lights around us [cheers]. When he says he 'cares not whether slavery is voted up or voted down'—that this is a sacred right of self-government—he is in my judgment penetrating the human soul and eradicating the light of reason and the love of liberty in the American people."

From time to time during Douglas's rebuttal, Mr. Lincoln would protestingly interrupt and had to be cautioned by his managers to remain quiet. The Judge became increasingly taunting and personal. By way of conclusion Douglas said: "He [Lincoln] does not want to avow his principles. I do want to avow mine, as clear as sunlight in mid-day [cheers and applause]. Democracy is founded upon the eternal principle of right. The plainer these principles are avowed before the people, the stronger will be the support they will receive. I only wish I had the power to make them so clear that they would shine in the heavens for every man, woman and child to read. The first of these principles that I would proclaim would be in opposition to Lincoln's doctrine of uniformity between the different States, and I would declare instead the sovereign right of each State to decide the slavery question as well as all other domestic questions for themselves, without any interference from any other State or power whatsoever."

The first of the "great" debates was over.

But not the excitement. When Douglas stepped down from the platform, amid Democratic vociferation, he was immediately surrounded by thousands of his faction, who with music, cheers and every demonstration of affectionate admiration followed him to his quarters in the hotel where, for several minutes they made the welkin ring with cheers and applause. The Judge took an early train for Chicago.

Lincoln's experience, although less dignified, was not dissimilar. He was hoisted onto the shoulders of two strong young farmers and in the center of a throng of some five thousand elated Republicans was paraded through the streets behind a band blaring *Hail Columbia*. Mr. Lincoln was really a ludicrous sight, holding frantically onto the heads of his supporters, with his legs dangling from their shoulders, and his pantaloons pulled up so as to expose his long underwear almost to his knees. It reminded him of one of his favorite stories about a man who was being ridden out of town on a rail who turned to his bearers and groaned: "If it wasn't for the honor of the thing, I'd rather walk."

Mr. Lincoln has thus been given the victor's treatment and this is disturbing to the Democratic press. The correspondent of the Chicago *Times,* in an effort to play down its implications, has included the following version of the incident in his dispatch: "Lincoln . . . seemed to have been paralyzed. He stood upon the stage looking wildly at the people as they surrounded the triumphant Douglas and, with mouth wide open, he could not find a friend to say one word to him in his distress. It was a delicate point for Republicans who had witnessed his utter defeat, and who knew how severely he felt it, to offer him condolence, or bid him hope for better success again. The only thing they could say was that Lincoln ought not to travel round with Douglas, and had better not meet him any more. When Douglas and the Democrats had left the square, Lincoln essayed to descend from the stage, but his limbs refused to do their office. During Douglas's last speech Lincoln had suffered severely; alternately burning with fever, and then suddenly chilled with shame, his respiratory organs had become obstructed, his limbs got cold, and he was unable to walk. In this extremity, the Republican Marshal called half a dozen men who, lifting Lincoln in their arms, carried him along. By some mismanagement the men selected for this office happened to be very short in stature, and the consequence was, that while Lincoln's head and shoulders towered above theirs, his feet dragged on the ground. Such an exhibition as the 'toting' of Lincoln from the square to his lodgings was never seen at Ottawa before. It was one of the richest farces we have ever witnessed, and provoked the laughter of all, Democrats and Republicans, who happened to see it." Mr. Lincoln will nail this distortion at a time and place of his own choosing.

Tonight there are bonfires and torchlight processions in Ottawa. Immediately after supper a large delegation of Republicans came to Mayor Glover's house, headed by a band of music, and escorted Mr. Lincoln and Owen Lovejoy, candidate for Congress, to the Court House. The building was brilliantly lighted, and a crowd, estimated to contain fifteen hundred persons, filled the yard in front. Lovejoy, who had promised to speak, was loudly called for, and, mounting the steps of the Court House, divested himself of his cravat and collar, opened his vest and shirt, and went at it.

When asked for comment on the day's activity, Mr. Lincoln replied: "The fire flew some, and I am glad to know that I am yet alive."

The second debate between Lincoln and Douglas will take place at Freeport on August 27.

Who in Triumph Advances

MR. LINCOLN'S route, to be sure, was circuitous and bore to the shortest distance between two points, or the flight of a crow, no discernible resemblance whatever. Still, in the minds of those sages, his self-appointed counselors, there were offsetting and superior advantages derivable from showing himself to as many of his passionate partisans as possible along the way. This unknown prodigy of the prairies might, moreover, by placing himself on public exhibition win over some of those whose enthusiasm for him and for his cause had been outwardly at least most magnificently concealed. Even so, many bids for his presence had had to be declined. The President-elect had been already on his way eastward for ten days and had not yet reached journey's end.

At the beginning of the month, that splendid Quaker, Charles S. Olden, had written from the Executive Department, "In compliance with the request of the Legislature of this State, I have sincere pleasure in extending to you an invitation to visit our State Capital . . . and affording the citizens of New Jersey an opportunity to express the respect they feel for your character and position." Five days later Mr. Lincoln had dispatched his acceptance, "with much gratitude to you and them for the kindness and honor thus offered." He had added a postcript: "Please arrange no ceremonies that will waste time."

Mr. Lincoln's hours would extend to almost half a million but the seven he gave to New Jersey would be among the most completely documented and the most vivid of them all. More importantly, they would be happier than those he would pass so soon. His journey from Springfield was a triumphal progress and seemed to culminate in the great ovation in New York. So crowded were the planned festivities in Manhattan that Mr. Lincoln was obliged to decline the hospitalities of Mr. John J. Chetwood, of Elizabeth. Mr. Chetwood had suggested "that you and your family, when you come on to the inauguration will make my house your house. I am within half an hour of N[ew] York, and a few hours of Washington, to which there are several trains daily. My house is large enough for you all, and you can be as retired as you wish. New Jersey you know is safe conservative ground." But Abraham Lincoln had become a public figure; there would be no seclusion for a while.

At eight o'clock on the morning of Thursday, February 21, he, his family and party emerged from the private entrance of the Astor House. For a moment he stood on the pavement, shaking hands with his hosts and repeatedly expressing gratification at the courtesies he had received. Then he climbed into his carriage and the procession clattered down to the foot of Cortlandt Street.

Despite the fact that it was almost an hour earlier than the time announced for his departure, there had been cheering along the way and a little company now stood on the dock to see him off. There was a short wait, while the elegant new ferryboat, the *John P. Jackson,* gay with streamers and bearing the welcomers from Jersey, was made fast. Then, when the plank had been lowered, the Presidential carriage drove on board, and Allen Dodworth's excellent band began to play. What it played is uncertain. It is generally agreed that it played "Hail," but the reporter of the *New York World* heard "Hail Columbia," while the man from Newark's *Sentinel of Freedom* listened to "Hail to the Chief."

Mr. Lincoln alighted from his carriage, and the moorings were cast off. Instead of taking the direct course, the pilot headed down the bay toward Bedloe's Island. Mr. Lincoln was escorted to the ladies' cabin where he was subjected to a greeting from A. A. Hardenbergh, president of the Board of Aldermen. "Sir," he said, "we are commissioned on behalf of the municipal authorities of Jersey City to receive and escort you to the soil of New Jersey." He spoke of "the high respect so eminently due to the chosen chief of a mighty people." He alluded to Mr. Lincoln's expedition "to assume the chair of Washington."

As for Jerseymen, Mr. Hardenbergh had this assurance: "Devoted in their attachment to the Union of these States, they cling to it with unchanging fidelity, as the ark of their political safety. It is their prayer that the Republic may be immortal, and that He who controls alike the destinies of individuals and nations may guide and sustain you, Mr. Lincoln, in all your course for the conservation of the public weal."

Then, presumably running out of words, Mr. Hardenbergh concluded: "Welcome, thrice welcome to the soil

of New Jersey!" Mr. Lincoln did not dissent from the
sentiment, he merely bowed his acknowledgment, but he
must have wondered how Mr. Hardenbergh reconciled
the soil of New Jersey to the fact that they were then
afloat on the water. It may have been a matter of riparian
rights.

The ladies were brought forward and introduced, and
Mr. Lincoln committed an exceptional act of gallantry.
One journalist recorded it this way: "Miss Annie Smith,
being more fortunate (as some thought) than the others,
was honored with a kiss." Had that newshawk been less
abstruse and more prophetic he might have noted that
Mr. Lincoln had performed a ritual and established a
precedent binding upon his successors to the latest generation: Annie was a babe-in-arms.

During a portion of the trip, Mr. Lincoln stood on the
deck, silently watching the receding skyline, the ripples
of the water, the cloudless heavens. A poet, nearby,
watched how "in the pursuing brightness of ten thousand eyes the dawn of the morning yielded to perfect
day," and hoped that it might be an earnest "of blessings
shortly to beam upon the nation."

Continuously the band played patriotic airs, the harbor
was animate with steamers, merchant ships, tugboats and
schooners, shooting athwart each other's track; "sturdy
sailors in seamen's accoutrements waved their tarpaulins
from shrouds . . . and perches." Mr. Lincoln was enraptured. He confided a hope of one day enjoying "a
fuller and more extended view" of the harbor.

As the *John P. Jackson* neared the dock, a detachment
of Hudson County Artillery, stationed north of the depot,
fired a salute of thirty-four guns; and the Cunarders,

Africa and *Jura,* lying at their wharf, dressed for the occasion, completely covered from decks to mastheads with stars and stripes and union jacks "mingling in harmonious profusion," sent up an echoing salvo. In a moment, Mr. Lincoln was conducted on shore by Alderman Hardenbergh, followed by members of the committee, and was shaking hands with Mayor Van Vorst. Abraham Lincoln had made his first appearance in what he called "Old Jersey."

The Mayor took Mr. Lincoln by the arm and led him into the depot of the New Jersey Railroad Company. It was an imposing structure of envied and "mammoth magnitude." The gallery which surrounded the interior had been reserved for the exclusive occupancy of ladies, and was packed. Gentlemen thronged the floor. Those who could not gain admittance to the building worked their way to the roof and "contented themselves with a bird's eye view through the skylights." Its capacity was said to be ten thousand but twenty-five thousand had come to witness the proceedings. On a track, in the center, a "platform car" had been converted to a stage. It was "carpeted and hung with red, white and blue trimmings." The appearance of Mr. Lincoln was the "signal for protracted cheering almost drowning the music" of the band. Mr. Lincoln was conducted to the platform.

Governor Olden could not be present; he was in Washington attending a futile Peace Convention. In his stead, he had sent that man without reproach, William L. Dayton. Four years before, in the first Republican campaign he had run for the Vice Presidency on the ticket headed by John Charles Fremont. At the recent convention at Chicago he had been one of the contenders for nomina-

tion to the highest office in the land. He was now Governor Olden's Attorney General; he would be Mr. Lincoln's
Minister to France.

Addressing Mr. Lincoln, General Dayton began by
saying that the guest was welcome "to the hearts and
homes of our citizens." Somewhat deprecatingly, he continued: "We may not hope to equal the magnificence of
the ovation which has attended your course to the capital." He was sure, however, that "in cordiality we are
second to none." There was enthusiastic applause when
he affirmed that "We have assembled to testify to our
appreciation of your character, our unwavering loyalty
to the laws and the Constitution, and our devotion to
the great interests of our country and the perpetuity of
the Union." It was the desire of his fellow citizens "to
live in harmony with all. The people of New Jersey prefer one country, one flag, one destiny." Then, looking
straight at Mr. Lincoln, he said: "Upon you, sir, upon
whom so much depends, we feel that we may depend, at
least for rectitude of intentions. The people will attend
you . . . with their fondest hopes, their best wishes, and
their prayers."

Thereafter "it was some moments before the enthusiastic" shouts of approval "subsided sufficiently" to permit Mr. Lincoln to reply. He stood there gaunt and waiting. Then, at last, with that simple, halting manner,
sometimes discoverable in his extemporaneous utterances,
he acknowledged the tribute of the foremost Jerseyman:

Ladies and gentlemen . . . I shall only thank you briefly
for this very kind and cordial reception, given not to me
personally, but to the temporary representative of the chief

magistracy of the nation. In the kindness of the people, I shall be frequently met to-day as I am here, and time will not permit me to do more than express my thanks for your reception, and briefly to say farewell. You have done me the distinguished honor to extend your welcome through your great man, one whom it would be a pleasure to me to meet anywhere, and no State which possesses such a man can ever be poor.

That brought down the house. His orator's instinct told him to wind it up. "It would require an hour, in a well-considered address," he said, on the verge of a split infinitive, "to properly reply to his brief speech, and I can only say that I heartily respond to and endorse all that he has said. Allow me most kindly to bid you farewell."

At that point "the cheering was revived, after which there were loud cries for Vice President Hamlin." It was announced that Hannibal had been detained in New York. Then the crowd insisted on an encore from Mr. Lincoln. Smiling broadly, he complied: "There appears to be a desire to see more of me, and I can only say that from my position, especially when I look around the gallery [*bowing to the ladies*], I feel that I have decidedly the best of the bargain, and in this matter I am for no compromises here."

The audience laughed, and "a son of Hibernia, of small stature, but great breadth of shoulders and resoluteness of purpose, managed to climb upon the platform and secure the hand of Mr. Lincoln, which he shook with more than ordinary Celtic enthusiasm. A policeman made free with the dwarfish son of Erin, and with his club punched him off the platform to the great delectation of the crowd."

The enthusiast was unabashed. "I got a shake of his hand," he insisted, "I am satisfied"; and Mr. Lincoln, nudging Mayor Van Vorst, remarked that "He is not the first one who, by the pressure of unforeseen circumstances has been compelled to desert his platform."

Mr. Lincoln then boarded his car, and precisely at eight-fifty-five o'clock "the steam whistle gave several shrill shrieks, the locomotive began the puffs premonitory of motion, and, amid the cheers of the crowd, 'Hail Columbia' by the band, and a cannon salute of thirty-four guns, the train started from the depot."

The train must have presented an extraordinay spectacle. It was drawn by engine No. 2, named for one of the Governors Pennington, a silken star affixed to the front of its boiler, its sides embellished with flags and flowers. Behind it, says one report, was coupled a smoker, set apart for the accommodation of "smaller fry politicians, disappointed in the hope of a confidential interview with his Excellency . . . where their despair was stifled in clouds of opiate smoke." Behind it came two elegantly appointed parlor cars, one of which had lately been commissioned for the transport of the Prince of Wales during his recent visit.

The car provided for Mr. Lincoln was particularly elaborate. It was "decorated with small flags over the front and rear windows, and with festoons and rosettes of the national colors and bunting. Four lounges, two marble-topped tables, with half a dozen ordinary seats, formed the furniture . . . On one table a gorgeous bouquet, in an oval basket, shed fragrance on the air—on the other table a large salver-pitcher and goblets of solid silver were placed." It was "richly carpeted and warmed with patent hot air furnaces with self-acting registers." The walls were covered with "mirrors and handsome engravings." This was described as being the "hindmost" car.

The middle car was almost equally resplendent. It, too, was handsomely fitted with tapestry, carpet, lounges, armchairs, and a center table on top of which flowers were beautifully disposed in a basin. The arrangements were the work of a Mr. Baker, Superintendent of Cars.

It is reported that the train "steamed cautiously toward Newark." Every precaution had been taken. "Flag men were stationed at all the prominent crossings, and the regular mail line preceded the train by a few minutes, so that any embarrassment might not remain to delay the President-elect." Places "overlooking the road were thronged with men and women. They had climbed into trees and upon roofs, wherefrom continuous shouts rang up, deafening the noise of the train."

An observant passenger, notebook in hand, set down his impressions:

On the rear seat, adjacent to the door leading to the rear platform, sat the President elect. Mrs. Lincoln, her sister Mrs. Edwards, the children, and Robert Lincoln, the eldest son, surrounded him. One of the juvenile Lincolns [it must have been Tad] carried a small flag, which he took great delight in waving at sundry times. He was a handsome little fellow, with a face of good humor, ever bordering upon a laugh, and his childish interest in the scenes through which he was passing gave animation to his eye and face, strangely contrasting with the serious bent of his father's brow, evidently grave above thoughts and feelings. For Lincoln the younger, there were tints in the clouds and a pleasant sunshine in all the slopes and streams . . . Abraham Lincoln was silent, perhaps even moody. Such was well, for flippancy, or a leer, upon the forehead of the man to whom all eyes in the nation look, would have ill assorted with the somber time and his solemn trusts. We remarked, along the entire route, that while the clamors of citizens betrayed him often into publicity, and sometimes even into words, at no time were there evidences in his eye of unworthy gratification forgetful of the general clouds in his own sunshine. Mr. Lincoln, so far as we could observe, was ever the man of genial dignity. There was nothing of the demagogue in any word, movement, or expression. No cynic could have justly found anything to reprove; he was no longer "Uncle Abe the Railsplitter," or even "Abe Lincoln" or, more respectfully, "Lincoln," but the President Elect, bearing the dignity of his office, and yet abating nothing of that uniform cordiality which has made his name a synonym of kindness.

On schedule to the minute, the Lincoln Special reached Newark's Morris & Essex Station at half-past nine. Everything was in readiness for his coming. Two days before a committee had called on him at the Astor House. He had made but one personal request: "no speeches, introductions or hand-shakings." Details had been worked out with Mr. W. S. Wood, superintendent of the Lincoln itinerary. The Committee had announced that the President-elect would pass through the city from the Morris & Essex Railroad Station to the Chestnut Street Station, a mile and a half away, by way of Broad Street, where citizens were asked to take their positions away from the depots, in order that they might see the procession without interference with the line. Division Street and Chestnut Street below Mulberry would be kept clear of all persons and vehicles except the carriages provided for the guests. It had been necessary to decline General Runyon's proffer of his brigade because there would be no time for march-

ing the militia. It was desirable that there should be no
partisan exhibition of banners. Mr. Lincoln would be
visiting Newark not as a Republican but as President-
elect.

Let me repeat: Mr. Lincoln had asked that there should
be no speeches, introductions or hand-shakings, but
when he and General Dayton stepped from the car, Judge
Cleaver, of the Common Council, presented Mayor Bige-
low who felt compelled to honor the request by breach-
ing it. He welcomed Mr. Lincoln to "the metropolis of
the State" and told him that its citizens "have ever been
loyal to the Constitution and maintained the integrity
of the Union, and . . . entertain an ardent hope that
your administration will be governed by that wisdom and
by that discretion which will be the means of transmitting
the confederated States, as a unit to your successors."

Mr. Lincoln listened with fixed attention. There must
have been an expression on the faces of the men and
women around him which somehow reminded him of
home and of far-off, familiar comparisons, for when his
turn came, he paraphrased the words he had spoken ten
days before. "Mr. Mayor," he said, "I thank you for this
kind reception to your city, and would say in response
that my heart is sincerely devoted to the work you desire I should do. With my own ability I cannot hope to
succeed, but I trust to be sustained by Divine Providence,
and this great, free, happy and intelligent people. Without this I cannot hope to succeed; with it, I cannot fail."

There were cheers then and again when he entered
the barouche, owned by Mr. Samuel Meeker, President
of the State Bank. Hitched to it were four gray horses.
The driver was I. Halsey Snyder. The Mayor, Judge

Cleaver and General Dayton occupied seats beside the President-elect. Headed by a company of horsemen the procession of twenty carriages began to move.

Since early morning the streets had been almost impassable. Hackensack, Paterson, Elizabeth, "and a hundred little villages" had "sent their quota of spectators. Balconies and windows were crowded; vehicles of all possible patterns" had "rattled into town; the ladies" had "collected their choicest bouquets to welcome the anticipated guest." According to one newspaper account, "It seemed as though [the] entire population of half the state had gone wild with enthusiasm and delight. The people ran, shouted, hurraed, and waved hats and handkerchiefs to an astonishing degree. The roofs of stores, dwellings, factories and sheds were covered with nearly as many spectators as were in the streets."

Another journalist was even more amazed; he wrote that "Men, women, and children were temporarily insane. The ladies from their perches scattered flowers and threw kisses; the hoarse throats of the men roared cheer after cheer; all the city was in the streets and the streets could not have known themselves, so wild was the delight. Thousands of feet tramped after the carriage; the esteem of the citizens appeared to amount to worship; men wandered from their wits, and cried they knew not what."

Mr. Lincoln remarked that he himself had known no such rival exultation since his departure from Springfield. Along the way, flags were everywhere displayed. Mr. Cummings had placarded his fruit store with letters spelling "Welcome." Dave's dry goods store was decked in red, white and blue ribbons. McGregor, the clothier, displayed the national ensign. Mr. Lincoln spoke to his companions, commenting on the beautiful elms of the park, the population of the city, and some of its great statesmen. In front of his store, at 344 Broad Street, near the City Hotel, Roswell W. Holmes, merchant tailor, had hit upon an unusual way of displaying his wares, by suspending the effigy of a man with a long black beard bearing a whip in his nerveless hand. Beneath swung a board bearing the legend, "The Doom of Traitors." Some said the figure represented John Brown; others, that he was a Black Republican; while others held that it was nothing more than a slave-beating secessionist. Members of Mr. Lincoln's suite regarded it with evident distaste, but himself "took but a passing notice" of it. After all he had been hung in effigy himself.

At the Ninth Ward Public School, the students were arranged on three platforms—one of them adorned with "an elegant silk flag." When Mr. Lincoln passed, "the school sang 'Hail Columbia,' which the President acknowledged by rising and bowing three times." As the procession neared the Chestnut Street Station the crowds broke through the police lines and actually hemmed it in. A body of horsemen was compelled to ride through the mass, and even then the merest lane was opened. So great was the rush of the crowd that several persons were thrown down and trampled. One Thomas Winton had his collarbone broken.

When, with the assistance of Police Lieutenants Garrabrant and Rowe, Mr. Lincoln finally gained the station, he immediately boarded the train. From the rear platform his friend from Elizabeth, Mr. Chetwood, introduced him to the concourse of persons who jammed the

building. Mr. Lincoln bowed, thanked them for the complimentary turnout and went inside. At ten-thirty-five,
to the strains of "The Star-Spangled Banner" he was on
his way again. It began to snow.

Rahway was reached at 10:40. There, DeGraw's Hotel
had been put in readiness to receive him, but "owing to
fatigue" Mr. Lincoln "was forced to decline the invitation to leave the train. He merely appeared for a moment
without offering any remarks." At New Brunswick there
was a pause long enough to permit Judge Van Dyke, of
the Supreme Court, to deliver a welcoming address and
to receive a polite statement in return. There, as at Elizabeth and Rahway, guns were fired "whose echo was heard
as the train rattled into the open country."

At Princeton the students were out in force. It is recorded that as the train passed through their reception
was featured by the ear-splitting sky-rocket cheer, and
that Mr. Lincoln went out on the "hinder platform" to
bow to them. When the excursion train which followed
the Lincoln Special, drawn by a locomotive bearing Mr.
Chetwood's name, arrived, many Princetonians boarded
it and "pursued" Mr. Lincoln noisily singing "Gaudea-
mus Igitur."

The climax of his New Jersey expedition came for Mr.
Lincoln at the State Capital. The train reached Trenton
at eleven-fifty. The sun was out again and the city was in
holiday humor. Parties had come from Belvidere, Burlington, Lambertville, Easton and all the neighboring
communities. Many of the gentlemen in the crowd about
the station had made his advent the occasion for a binge.
In a nearby beer parlor his warm adherent, Christopher
Gerber had bet "that he could do what no Democrat

could." His challenge had been accepted, and Chris "first lifted twelve times in succession at arms'-length, above his head, a keg of lager." Then he "lifted it twelve times from the floor with his teeth." It is said that he won the wager.

Druggists did a lively business in the English Doctor Bellingham's preparation; a stimulating ointment "warranted to bring out a thick set of whiskers or a moustache in from three to six weeks."

Along the route the gendarmerie had been effective and stouthearted. That could not be said of Trenton's "finest." Indeed, a reporter left this dismal recollection.

The policemen of Trenton [he wrote] reminded us of the starred gentry employed at Camac's Woods on the occasion of Mr. Heenan's champion benefit. Some of them were lame; one or two were blind, and several prepared themselves for usefulness by getting inebriated at an early hour. Most of them carried canes, and in deficiency of wardrobe and general dilapidation of hats and boots, they rivalled Pistol, Bardolph & Co. To these lawful folk we are indebted, with other strangers, for sundry gougings, shakings, and violent cuffs acquired in the discharge of our reportorial duties.

Perhaps they presented an invitation to crime. In any event pickpockets made off with about five thousand dollars, and for days thereafter the local press would contain items like this:

"A pocket-book containing papers, receipts &c., of S. Gillam who was one of the sufferers on Thursday last, has been left with John Ashmore, Janitor of the City Hall."

Or like this:

"The pocket-book of Ira Johnson, tax collector of Hamilton township, was found by a little boy in an outhouse on Mr. Housel's place in Greene Street, and has been left at the Mayor's office." Surely it was a memorable day for Trenton!

Mr. Lincoln stepped from the train and was introduced by General Dayton to Mayor Mills. His Honor gave forth with words of gracious welcome which differed in no important particular from others heard that morning. Mr. Lincoln by way of answer "adverted to no political topic, but stated that he was proud to accept the hospitalities of the State of New Jersey." General Dayton carried Mrs. Lincoln and the boys off to his home for lunch, and the President-elect fell into line again behind the Paterson Blues and Trenton's German Rifles. As the cavalcade filed up State Street, "the propellers and vessels laying in the Trenton Basin had their flags and streamers flying." Private residences and places of business were decorated. The curious stood on the roofs of houses, in the rooms of the City Hall, and newspaper offices to watch the procession as it moved to the Capitol.

At twelve-fifteen, Mr. Lincoln, escorted by the Legislative Committee, appeared in the New Jersey Senate. That small chamber presented an attractive appearance. Strangers were confined to the lobbies situated considerably lower than the floor. Some highly privileged ladies sat in a little gallery just below, and adjacent to, the ceiling. The floor, where the Members sat, was kept clear. To this Mr. Lincoln was ushered. He stood, between his sponsors, gloved, slightly bending, but still a full head taller than any man about him; his shoulders seemed very broad. His head was thrust forward as he was introduced by Senator Cook to the President of the Senate, Mr. Perry. President Perry was eloquent. He concluded his short greeting with these words:

"That you may receive from on High, wisdom to direct and strength to sustain you in the discharge of the laborious duties of your high office, and that you may so succeed as to merit the universal plaudit of 'Well done, good and faithful servant,' is, I am sure, to-day, the prayer of millions of freemen. Go, honored sir, to your great task, and may God go with you."

It is obvious from the tone of Mr. Lincoln's reply that the day's exertions had tired him. Perhaps he rambled ever so little. It is hard to know, for the published reports do not agree as to the words he used. The text as reproduced in the *Daily Gazette and Republican* had probably been edited. Another, possibly more accurate version has him speaking this marathon sentence:

I am exceedingly anxious that that thing which they [the Continental Army] struggled for; that something even more than national independence; that something that held out a great promise to all the people of the world to all time to come; I am exceedingly anxious that this Union, the Constitution, and the liberties of the people shall be perpetuated in accordance with the original idea for which that struggle was made; and I shall be most happy, indeed, if I shall be an humble instrument in the hands of the Almighty, and of this, His chosen people for perpetuating the object of that great struggle.

At that point, on the motion of a Senator named Reckless, the Senate adjourned. Mr. Lincoln was then cast to the Assemblymen. There appears to have been confusion in the Assembly chamber. It is told how the "spectators

in the rear cried: 'Down in front,' and those in front
said 'sh-sh!' until the matter waxed exceedingly disorderly,
and the Speaker of the Chamber spoke, in order to drown
the strife.''

Speaker Teese (and what a name his was for a Speaker!)
felt constrained to dwell upon the gravity of the times.
He made it very clear that "the bravest, the wisest, and
the best stand still, in doubt and awe of the position of
our national affairs." He pledged Mr. Lincoln a qualified
allegiance.

He went on for a sentence or two and then subsided.

I am happy to give you, sir, the assurances of the descendants
of those whose blood was shed in the cause of liberty upon this
soil, of the continued devotion of this State to the Constitution and the Union founded by our fathers, and that our
people will heartily cooperate with you in all constitutional
efforts for a speedy and honorable settlement of the differences which now unhappily distract our country.

Meanwhile, Mr. Lincoln had had an opportunity to
recover his vigor and to determine upon the most signifi-
cant and outspoken statement he had made since his election. It is unnecessary to repeat it all. One who listened
said immediately afterward that there was "a conversa-
tional dignity" about it. "There was no fulsome humble-
ness in his manner of stating his unworthiness; but the
mildness of a man, not too fearless to be rash, and not so
fearful as prudent."

Mr. Lincoln declared, "the man does not live who is
more devoted to peace than I am; none who would do
more to preserve it; but it may be necessary to put the
foot down firmly." The auditor noted that when he re-

iterated his devotion to peace, there was kindness and truth in his bearing, but when he spoke of putting the foot down firmly, "his shoulders seemed to straighten and his eye to kindle. He stood so during the fierce applause, as if unconscious of any emotion save his own expressed resolution."

Then Mr. Lincoln continued: "And if I do my duty, and do right you will sustain me, will you not?" As he posed that question of mingled pathos and humor to his political opponents, his shoulders seemed visibly to relax and into his eye there stole "the softness of a child." The watcher believed that his was a *"naïveté* too powerful to be artful." The Assemblymen seem to have agreed. They shouted "Yes! Yes! We will!" Mr. Lincoln must have found confidence in their endorsement and have supposed it genuine.

Following his visit to the Capitol, Mr. Lincoln was driven to the Trenton House. There he was conducted to the second story, where a staging had been erected at one of the windows. Below, the military companies were drawn up on the pavement; behind them stood that great crowd. He thanked his New Jersey friends again for their goodness to him.

Mr. Lincoln then went downstairs to lunch. He was obliged to enter the dining room by way of the kitchen. This detour was necessitated by the throng which tussled with policemen in the doors, and surged fearfully in the halls and on the front stairways. About five hundred persons shared the "excellent collation" with Mr. Lincoln but he was the only guest provided with a chair.

When he had finished, he went to his room, and "in fifteen minutes was again seated in his private car, and being whirled at a rapid rate through South Trenton across the Delaware, and into Pennsylvania." Abraham Lincoln's first visit to New Jersey was over. It had been nice to be hailed as the Chief.

But before the weekend was out there would be disaffection among the Jerseymen. They would excoriate him for his clandestine entry into Washington. Rapidly, the Union would dissolve in Civil War, and where there was not raw sorrow, there would be the wasting, the deadening of disappointment. In the presidential elections, four years later, Jerseymen would give their vote to their favorite son, the displaced general, the defeatist candidate. Could Copperheads strike so hard?

Actually, of course, on that far-off Thursday when Abraham Lincoln crossed the Delaware, his days of greatness lay ahead. Those days and his greatness would be summed up, long after, by the begotten of that old Revolutionary, "Thumbs" Chambers, of the Hunterton County Militia. His findings would be that

The period of the presidency, the period when Abraham Lincoln matured and came to being, has escaped the microscopic examination which has been applied to his earlier, unexceptional career. It is because he was so much in and of his world that Abraham Lincoln is the foremost American. He is foremost because he was the central focal character in a bruising, bitter, wretched, splendid moment when many men were great and he was greater still. He is foremost because his contemporaries made him foremost, conceded his primacy, and conferred their power and their honor on him. In short, Abraham Lincoln stands alone in history largely because in life he stood among the people. Only through them, the inhabitants of a wide, broken, angry land, is it possible to find him. Their responses to him and his to them, their anguish and his sympathies, their aspirations and his endeavors, their reaching out and his upholding of them, are the strong roots from which his towering spirit grows.

If this is true (and I, for one, believe it) what then of the Jerseymen? Had the fires that Lincoln lit at New Brunswick and at Newark and at Trenton, been the pyres of his own destruction? Had their intensity consumed them? A writer in Newark's *Daily Advertiser* had found omen in the climate. He wrote, the next day, that "the weather, too, was suggestive of his political progress. The day opened with a bright sky, soon after obscured by frigid snow-squalls, and finally terminating in a clear invigorating atmosphere."

Perhaps that was it: perhaps the Jerseymen waited for the clearing. Mr. Lincoln had hardly passed through Rahway before a charming opera singer, writing in broken English, had besought him to take up the mortgage on her villa there. Even earlier, two girls of Irvington had adopted him as their brother. There had been the man in New Brunswick who had worn out his boots in the campaign and now asked Mr. Lincoln to buy him another pair. There had been the man in Orange who solicited compensation for injuries incurred in firing a cannon to celebrate the election.

Mr. Lincoln's second coming to New Jersey was in the early summer of 1862. He had journeyed to West Point, there to consult with General Winfield Scott. At eleven o'clock, Wednesday morning, June 25, he stepped off the ferry at Jersey City, accompanied only by the aged General, Colonel Daniel Craig McCallum, military director of railroads, and a Negro servant. The President, "in excellent health and most cheerful spirits, was very plainly attired in a suit of black summer cloth, and rather dusty with travel."

General Scott said his good-byes and Mr. Lincoln boarded his two-car special train. But he had been recognized. About thirty persons gathered around the car calling for a speech. In response, he explained that he had not gone to West Point because of any sudden exigency, nor any difficulty in National affairs beyond what they all knew as well as he did; nor had he gone for the purpose of "making or unmaking" generals. Having thus given them the negative objects of his visit, he could only remind them that the Secretary of War, Mr. Stanton, held a very tight rein on the newspapers, adding, "if I should blab anything they cannot publish, I do not know what he will do with me." At that moment the whistle blew and the train moved out of the station. There were cheers. It was eight minutes after eleven. At ten minutes before seven that evening, Mr. Lincoln was back in Washington.

But when Mr. Lincoln was in the White House and the heat turned on, there was a diminution of that sublime confidence. In that period, Mr. Lincoln received some two hundred and fifty letters from Jerseymen and most are easily categorized: applications for place, appeals for clemency, instructions for the conduct of the war, criticism of policy. For a sable season, the Lincoln experience was suspended. The man was diffused in the Head of State.

Perhaps, for Jerseymen, as for his biographers, Nicolay and Hay, the President, as individual, was displaced in popular imagination by the more compelling, the nearer considerations of the War and the sacrifices a loyal people made to it. Certainly, the State's participation in it was exemplary and ennobled. It was called upon for 78,248 troops; it supplied 88,305, a surplus of 10,057. It paid $2,275, 989 to dependents and $23,000,000 in bounties. Two hospitals were established at Newark and one at Jersey City. There were national cemeteries at Beverly and Newark. Jerseymen who were killed or died in service numbered 218 officers and 6,082 enlisted men.

As for Mr. Lincoln, the College of New Jersey, now Princeton University, on December 20, 1864, conferred on him the honorary degree of Doctor of Laws. In his acknowledgment of the award Doctor Lincoln expressed himself as "thankful if my labors have seemed to conduce to the preservation of those institutions under which alone we can expect good government and in its train sound learning and the progress of the liberal arts."

Then, in the healing spring of 1865, the spirit of Lincoln broke through the mist. A gentleman at Caldwell wrote: "My appreciation of your kind attention to an individual case like mine, in the midst of your great responsibilities and cares, is great indeed—and I desire to repeat the assurance of the grateful sense we shall ever have of the consideration and parental sympathy which your action in this instance has evinced." From Mount Holly came this message: "May God bless you and your measures with complete and entire success." And from Hoboken, a veteran who had served two years in "Seward's Infantry," informed the President: "I have settled down in my avocation as Music Teacher and during my leisure moments composed a March. Always having been an ardent admirer of you and the principles you advocate,

I desire to dedicate the March to you, to be called the 'Lincoln March.' "

On April 24 Mr. Lincoln came back to Jersey City. Again the throngs were great. Again the station was suitably decorated. Again the Cunarders did him honor. But there was a difference and it was hushed. There was starkness in the announcement:

At Jersey City the assemblage was immense; but so admirable were all the arrangements that not a single disturbance or delay occurred in transferring the remains from the cars to the boat. The spacious depot of the New Jersey Rail Road Company was appropriately draped and exhibited several mottoes, one of which read

> GEORGE WASHINGTON THE FATHER
> ABRAHAM LINCOLN THE SAVIOR, OF OUR COUNTRY.

The remains of Lincoln! Could the black soil of Sangamon's Oak Ridge contain his essence? If it *could*, Mr. President, what are *we* doing here?

Abraham Lincoln
As a Purer Nelson

M O R E than once Carl Sandburg has been heard to say of Abraham Lincoln that "the son of a gun grows on you." Perhaps that is what Edwin Arlington Robinson differently expressed when he wrote that Lincoln was "elemental when he died." For certainly Lincoln is still growing. He is, as he described himself as a child, "large of his age." No one in America is larger and every age is his. As perspective lengthens so does he. Mr. Lincoln is, in height, no longer "six feet, four inches, nearly, weighing on an average one hundred and eighty pounds"; but a being taller and more ponderous.

It might be supposed that everything that could be or, should be, said of Mr. Lincoln had been said already. Happily that is not the case.

For it is the fashion nowadays for writers to expend tremendous stores of energy in proving how utterly mistaken, stupid and deluded their predecessor-rivals have been in representing Mr. Lincoln as having been this or that kind of a creature whereas, in reality, he was something else and very different; or in exposing forgeries

committed in his name; or in producing evidence which
flatly contradicts other evidence and leaves poor Abraham
a trembling blur. It is, for the writers, a pleasant pastime
which may, in the long run, even do some good. It is even
possible to give a practical demonstration of the formula.

In the third spring of the Civil War, Mr. Henry Tuckerman, of New York, sent to the press a formidable essay
entitled "America and Her Commentators." It contained
this sweeping statement:

Throughout our national sorrows, from the inception of
this wicked Rebellion, through all its course, the spirit of the
press and Parliament, the spirit of England, as far as it has
found official expression, with a few memorable exceptions,
have been unjust, disengenuous, and inimical; and when the
history of this national crisis is written, the evidence of this
will be as glaring as it is shameful.

Mr. Tuckerman took an especially dim view of the
behavior of the London *Times,* charged it with circu-
lating "wanton falsehoods," and declared "that hence-
forth the mechanical resources and intellectual appliances
of that famous newspaper weigh as nothing against the
infamy that attends a discovered quack."

These unqualified accusations invite attention. How
do they, for example, apply to the Lincoln experience?

Shortly after Mr. Lincoln's inauguration, a *Times* correspondent appeared in Washington. His name was William Howard Russell. In the Crimea he had attained an
excellent reputation as an objective reporter. At Bala-
clava he had invented a famous phrase, "the thin red
line," for the British Infantry, which Mr. Kipling would

one day borrow; and he had inspired the work of Miss Florence Nightingale. More recently he had covered the Indian Mutiny. Mr. Russell (he had not yet become Sir William) had been around.

On the morning of March 27, 1861, the Assistant Secretary of State took Mr. Russell to the White House, to watch the minister of the new kingdom of Italy present his credentials to the President. They were shown into "a handsome spacious room, richly and rather gorgeously furnished, and rejoicing in a kind of 'demi-jour,' which gave increased effect to the gilt chairs and ormolu ornaments." What ensued, Mr. Russell recorded in his diary:

Soon afterwards [he wrote] there entered, with a shambling, loose, irregular, almost unsteady gait, a tall, lank, lean man, considerably over six feet in height, with stooping shoulders, long pendulous arms, terminating in hands of extraordinary dimensions, which, however, were far exceeded in proportion by his feet. He was dressed in an ill-fitting, wrinkled suit of black, which put one in mind of an undertaker's uniform at a funeral; round his neck a rope of black silk was knotted in a large bulb, with flying ends projecting beyond the collar of his coat; his turned-down shirt collar disclosed a sinewy muscular yellow neck, and above that nestling in a great black mass of hair, bristling and compact like a ruff of mourning pins, rose the strange quaint face of Abraham Lincoln. The impression produced by the size of his extremities, and by his flapping and wide projecting ears, may be removed by the appearance of kindliness, sagacity, and the awkward bonhomie of his face; the mouth is absolutely prodigious; the lips, straggling and extending almost from one line of black beard to the other, are kept in order by two deep furrows from the nostril to the chin; the nose itself—a prominent organ—stands out from the face, with an inquiring, anxious air, as though it were sniffing for some good thing in the air.

So far the description bore out the Tuckerman accusa-
tion of British disrespect; the portrait could not be said
to be recklessly flattering, but at this point Mr. Lincoln
began to grow on Russell. The diarist continued:

The eyes dark, full, and deeply set, are penetrating, but
full of an expression which almost amounts to tenderness; and
above them projects the shaggy brow, running into the small
hard frontal space, the development of which can scarcely be
estimated accurately, owing to the irregular flocks of thick
black hair carelessly brushed across it. One would say that,
although the mouth was made to enjoy a joke, it could also
utter the severest sentence which the head could dictate, but
that Mr. Lincoln would be ever more willing to temper justice with mercy, and to enjoy what he considers the amenities
of life, than to take a harsh view of men's nature and of the
world.

When the diplomatic ceremonies were concluded, the
journalist was presented to the President. Said Mr. Lincoln:

Mr. Russell, I am very glad to make your acquaintance,
and to see you in this country. The London "Times" is one of
the great powers in the world,—in fact, I don't know anything
which has much more power,—except the Mississippi. I am
glad to know you as its minister.

Mr. Russell departed from the executive presence
"agreeably impressed with his shrewdness, humour, and
natural sagacity." But poor Russell. It would not be long
before he would run afoul of the Union military by truthfully reporting the conduct of the Federal forces at first
Bull Run. This, of course, was offensive to the War De-

partment which retaliated by canceling Russell's passes. He was obliged to abandon his American assignment.

Early in 1862, *Macmillan's Magazine* had a "Special Correspondent in America." *Macmillan's* was one of the most important British periodicals of the day. Among its contributors were Richard Doddridge (*Lorna Doone*) Blackmore, Carlyle, the Rossettis, the Kingleys, and Matthew Arnold. For a time the anonymity of the "Special Correspondent in America" was carefully preserved, but he was later identified as Edward Dicey, then in his early twenties, lately a graduate of Trinity College, Cambridge, where he took honors in mathematics and the classics. He was a friend to John Stuart Mill. Upon his arrival in the United States, Dicey proceeded to Washington where he was promptly presented to Mr. Lincoln. Perhaps you will agree that Dicey's description copies the pattern adopted by William Howard Russell the year before. Here it is:

To say that he [Lincoln] is ugly, is nothing; to add that his figure is grotesque, is to convey no adequate impression. Fancy a man six foot high, and thin *out* of proportion; with long boney arms and legs, which somehow seem to be always in the way; with great rugged furrowed hands, which grasp you like a vice when shaking yours; with a long scraggy neck, and a chest too narrow for the great arms at its side. Add to this figure a head, cocoa-nut-shaped and somewhat too small for such a stature, covered with rough, uncombed and uncombable hair, that stands out in every direction at once; a face furrowed, wrinkled, and indented, as though it had been scarred by vitriol; a high narrow forehead, and, sunk beneath bushy eyebrows; two bright, somewhat dreamy eyes, that seem to gaze through you without looking at you; a few irregular blotches of black bristly hair, in the place where beard

and whiskers ought to grow; a close-set, thin-lipped, stern
mouth, with two rows of large white teeth, and a nose and
ears which have been taken by mistake from a head of twice
the size. Clothe this figure, then, in a long, tight, badly-fitting
suit of black, creased, soiled, and puckered up at every
salient point of the figure (and every point *is* salient); put on
large ill-fitting boots, gloves too long for the long bony fingers,
and a fluffy hat, covered to the top with dusty puffy crape; and
then add to all this an air of strength, physical as well as
moral, and a strange look of dignity coupled with all this
grotesqueness; and you will have the impression left upon
me by Abraham Lincoln.

As to Mr. Lincoln's characteristics, Dicey was more
considerate; he wrote:

You would never say he was a gentleman; you would still
less say he was not one. There are some women about whom
no one ever thinks in connexion with beauty one way or the
other; and there are men to whom the epithet of gentleman-
like or ungentleman-like appears utterly incongruous; and of
such Mr. Lincoln is one. Still there is about him an utter
absence of pretension, and an evident desire to be courteous
to everybody, which is the essence, if not the outward form, of
good breeding. There is a softness, too, about his smile, and a
sparkle of dry humour about his eye, which redeem the expression of his face, and remind me more of the late Dr.
Arnold [of Rugby], as a child's recollection recalls him, than
any face I can call to mind.

Perhaps such reports of mediocrity were the basis of a
statement by Joseph Lemuel Chester, published in *Macmillan's* for October, 1862:

The record of Mr. Lincoln's future cannot, of course, be
here written; there is little doubt, however, that the military

element . . . and other weighty political causes, will effectu-
ally prevent his re-election to the post he now occupies; and
his destiny is probably to return to his old functions as a
member of the Illinois bar.

The tide of battle was running steadily against the
Lincoln fortunes. In the field disaster followed hard upon
disaster. It seemed that "the Union as it was" would never
be restored. Even so learned and usually farsighted a British scholar as Leslie Stephen wrote two months later:

No great man has as yet shown himself capable of concen-
trating the popular admiration, and standing as a symbol of
the cause. . . . President Lincoln is a benevolent elderly
gentleman with an unpleasant trick of setting his foot down
in the wrong place. . . . Neither Lincoln nor M'Clellan are
exactly qualified to stand as personifications of the strongest
aspirations of a great people.

But things were looking up for Mr. Lincoln when
Goldwin Smith, Royal Professor of History, at Oxford
University, came to see him on the morning of November
16, 1864. Mr. Lincoln had continued to grow on people;
he had continued to grow himself; there had been some
Federal victories; he had been re-elected to office; the
successful issue of the long, angry, bitter conflict was in
sight. Goldwin Smith took a hard look at the man before
him and noted that—

The President's face and figure are well known by likenesses
and caricatures. The large-boned and sinewy frame . . . is
probably that of the yeoman of the north of England—the
district from which Lincoln's name suggests that his ancestors
came—made spare and gaunt by the climate of America. The
face, in like manner, denotes an English yeoman's solidity of

character and good sense, with something superadded from the enterprising life and sharp habits of the Western Yankee. The brutal fidelity of the photograph, as usual, has given the features of the original, but left out the expression. It is one of kindness, and, except when specially moved to mirth, of seriousness and care. The manner and address are perfectly simple, modest, and unaffected, and therefore free from vulgarity in the eyes of all who are not vulgar themselves.

The harsh image had begun to soften, but when it came to the matter of Lincoln's genius, Goldwin Smith still had some reservations:

Whether he is a great man or not [he wrote], he is at least an honest one; he can feel responsibility; and his re-election was to be desired not only for the good of his own country, but for the peace of the world.

And Goldwin Smith came out stoutly in defense of the Lincoln personality, writing:

"A brutal boor" is the epithet applied to the twice-elected representative of the American nation by certain English journals and the assiduous repetition of this and equivalent phrases has probably fixed that idea of Mr. Lincoln in the minds of the unreflecting mass of our people. . . . That he is something more than a boor his address at the dedication of the cemetery at Gettysburg will in itself be sufficient to prove. . . . There are one or two phrases here, such as "dedicated to the proposition," which betray a hand untrained in fine writing, and are proofs that the composition is Lincoln's own. But looking at the substance, it may be doubted whether any king in Europe would have expressed himself more royally than the peasant's son. And, even as to the form, we cannot help remarking that simplicity of structure and pregnancy of meaning are the true characteristics of the classical style. Is it easy to believe that the man who had the native good taste to produce this address would be capable of committing gross indecencies—that he would call for comic songs to be sung over soldiers graves? . . . Chief of a party in one of the most desperate struggles of history, he has never, by anything that has fallen from his lips, gratuitously increased the bitterness of civil war. His answer to those who came to congratulate him on his re-election was thoroughly generous, chivalrous, and patriotic. He "did not wish to triumph over any man." He "had never wilfully planted a thorn in any man's bosom." It is true that he had not.

This appeared in *Macmillan's* for February, 1865. In June some familiar by-lines reappeared. Mr. Lincoln meanwhile had been murdered and his British commentators felt themselves compelled to re-assess his worth and re-examine his probable place in history. Edward Dicey reproached himself for his earlier and disparaging portrait; he wrote:

I was introduced to the President as "one of his enemies." "I did not know I had any enemies," was the answer; and I can still feel, as I write, the grip of that great boney hand held out to me in token of friendship. In my life I have seen a good number of men distinguished by their talents or their station, but I never saw any one, so apparently unconscious that this distinction conferred upon him any superiority, as Abraham Lincoln.

And Dicey went on to speculate:

I have often asked myself of late whether Mr. Lincoln was a great man or not. To this question I find it very hard to give an answer. If sterling goodness of heart, wonderful native shrewdness, and an unflinching resolution to do what was just and right, constitute greatness, then the victim of Wilkes

Booth's crime was a very great man indeed. But if something other—though not perhaps higher—than all this is wanted to imprint upon a man the stamp of absolute greatness, then I still doubt whether the verdict of posterity will place Lincoln in the category of men who have made history. His real merit, in my judgment was that he represented so faithfully the people who had chosen him for their ruler. . . . A saviour of society, a Napoleon or a Cromwell, or even a Cavour, was not needed at this crisis of American history. All that was required was a man honest enough to resist temptation, resolute enough to carry out his purpose, shrewd enough to see his end clear before him and follow none other, and single-hearted enough to seek the welfare of the country, and that only. All these requisites were found in "Honest Abe" . . . I do not believe the last President was in any sense a man of genius. His record is grand and noble enough without our needing to attribute to him qualities which he did not possess. A purer Nelson, a wiser Garibaldi; his name will, if I mistake not, be cherished by the American people much as the memories of the two heroes I have mentioned are honored in their countries. Not only "in our island story" has the way of duty been found also to be the path of glory. We heard much, not so long ago, of the degeneracy of the nation which once was worthy to be led by Washington. History, I think, will say that our own days produced a yet nobler representative of American courage, and honesty, and self-sacrifice in the person of Abraham Lincoln.

Like Dicey, Professor Goldwin Smith declined an orgy of adulation and indulgence in ecstatic eulogy; in measured tones of self-imposed restraint he wrote:

In . . . [Lincoln] his nation has lost not a king or a prophet—not a creative moulder of its destinies or an inspired unfolder of its future—but simply a sensible interpreter and a wise, temperate, honest executor of its better mind. No popular chief has played so great a part since Cromwell. But the difference between Cromwell and Lincoln is the difference between an era of great men and an era of great nations.

And Goldwin Smith, dispensing justice, went on to pronounce this judgment:

The glory of Lincoln, like that of Washington, has nothing in it dazzling or grandiose; it is the quiet halo which rests round the upright, self-devoted, unwavering and unwearying performance of the hardest public duty. But its quiet light will shine steadily when many a meteor that has flamed in history has been turned, by the judgment of a sounder morality to darkness.

But there is no need to pursue the inquiry. Tuckerman's strictures on the British press have been corrected; his unfriendly generalities have been set aside. As Americans we can settle with the English newsmen for "a purer Nelson," and for a "quiet halo" on a "cocoa-nut-shaped" head. For this much I submit: they *have* admitted that "the son of a gun grows on you."

The President and
the Princess

FROM the vantage of our after-time it is difficult to realize that not all of the women who thrummed and throved
in the Civil War were necessarily and singularly unattrac-
tive. We have it on the authority of Agnes (for such was
the first of the series of given names sported by the Princess)— We have it on the authority of Agnes herself that:

Congress, and especially the Senate, was the spring of grace,
and whoever had friends in that august body were sure of
success. In consequence of this many people who wanted some
favour from the Government crowded into Washington, and
amongst them the fair sex was strongly represented. In fact,
there were lady-politicians and lady-lobbyists, who made it a
business to exert the influence which they gained by their
coquetry over influential men, for the benefit not only of
their husbands or friends, but even for strangers and for ready
cash! Of course these ladies were neither old, nor ugly, nor
very prudish, and not much respected; but as society at that
time had more an eye to gain than to virtue, these ladies in
Washington were not aware of the contempt in which they
were held in other parts of the Republic. Washington was
then reputed as a most wicked and dissipating place, and

ladies that could not afford to pay it a visit shuddered at its
wickedness, whilst it was the highest desire of all the rest,
especially if good-looking, to pass a season in that abominable
place.

It would be interesting to know whether Agnes considered herself a member of that raptuous sorority. Unfortunately her origins, as usually reported, are defiantly
conflicting or obscure. With some confidence it may be
said that she was, in a most literal sense, a daughter of joy;
thereafter positive assurance totters and embarrassedly
disappears. Thus, for example, a romantic writer for the
Metropolitan Magazine once announced that: "Agnes Leclercq Joye [sic] was the daughter of a wealthy farmer
of Vermont, a man who boasted of being a descendant of
the early settlers of this country. The father and mother
died, leaving a large family of growing children who were
taken in charge by an older sister, who possessed all the
stern characteristics of the father without the counter-
acting tenderness of the mother. Agnes ran wild on the
great farm. She was from the first a rebel against her
sister's authority in such matters as being 'lady-like' according to the established standard of the little town. She
persisted in climbing trees and breaking the ponies at the
risk of breaking her own neck, and soon established the
reputation of being the most daring rider in the district.
At the outbreak of the war the beautiful, impulsive girl
of fifteen happened to be visiting friends in Washington."
On the other hand, the majestically factual *Dictionary
of American Biography,* wherein she is admitted to immortality, candidly confesses that she "was born [Decem-
ber 25, 1840] on a farm in Franklin County, Vt., or pos-

sibly in Philipsburg, Que., where part of her girlhood was spent. The daughter of William and Julia (Willard) Joy and the grand-daughter of Micah Joy, a Revolutionary soldier, she was descended from Thomas Joy," a colonial architect and builder. But the author of the sketch —a relative—passed hurriedly over her formative years, writing only that "her adventurous spirit which found vent in escapades which lived long in local tradition took her to Washington early in the Civil War."

But, strangely, it remained for Noah Brooks, correspondent of the *Sacramento Union* and Mr. Lincoln's consistent confidant, to paint her past in scarlet. The basis of his animus is curious and unclear. It may, of course, have reflected a distaste or disapproval personally and directly derived, or, again, it may have been vicariously transmitted through blushing loyalties. It is, however, a fact that several times in his writings he returned to the subject of Agnes and always to her disadvantage. Once, indeed, he devoted an entire article to her rise and progress, writing, in 1870:

When I knew her in Washington, during the War of the Rebellion, there ran a story that she had been picked up in Europe by the invalid wife of an American Cabinet Minister, who, fascinated by the child's beauty and winning ways, took her out of the streets of Paris and brought her home to Philadelphia. The good lady dying soon after her return to the United States, the wayward beauty gave her protector, the Cabinet Minister, no end of trouble in consequence of her eccentric escapades and pranks. Arriving at womanhood, she suddenly left her adopted home, where she had been surrounded with every luxury, but where the restraints of respectability had been too severe for her, and went to New York. She had received a good education . . . and from a child was mistress of several European languages. She claimed American parentage, but was Italian in personal appearance, French in manner and spirit, and decidedly Bohemian in her tastes. When in the prime of her young womanhood she was a very beautiful person, and as charming as beautiful. Her face was oval, with regular, but unclassic features and profile, dark chestnut eyes, a delicate and finely-molded chin and mouth, dark, wavy hair, and a singularly brilliant and winsome smile. In brief she was a fascinating little woman, perfectly bewitching where she determined to bewitch, and never sullen, grave, or morose to any body. . . . She was often more like a sprite than a woman of flesh and blood. If she had any furious temper concealed beneath this charming exterior, it never broke out, except on extraordinary occasions of severe provocation. But probably the volcano always slept there, though the sunny vines and flowers grew so prettily outside.

According to Brooks, she called herself, for reasons of her own, Alice Leclercq and was—

passionately fond of horses, horseback riding, and every thing thereunto pertaining. . . . It was natural enough that she should be enamored of the circus. The sawdust ring, the spangled splendors of the performers, the glamour of the gas-lights, so charmed her fancy that she drifted back to Philadelphia, in 1857, and besought the manager of a circus then established there to give her facilities for instruction in equestrianism and equitation. She applied herself assiduously . . . [but] notwithstanding . . . she failed as a circus-rider, and, tearfully, giving up her desire, she never appeared in public in that line of business. Her experience, however, suggested the idea of practicing the art of walking on the slack wire. In this she excelled . . . At Chicago, in the spring of 1858, she made her first public appearance as a "great ascensionist." Desirous of achieving fame, as well as adding to the attractions of the establishment to which she belonged, she resolved to ascend a stout wire, stretched from the ground to the exterior flag-staff of the circus-tent. The day was raw, chilly, and windy, when the girl, clad in pink and silver muslin, attempted the perilous ascent. The wind puffed vigorously at the lithe and agile body; the frail support swayed to and fro as the gusts clutched her short skirts, and, dropping her balance-pole, she fell, like a feather, into the horror-stricken crowd below. A stout acrobat, belonging to the company, had cautiously followed her on the ground, and she fell, unhurt, into his ready arms. Nothing daunted, she took her pole again, and, after a moment's breathing-spell, walked safely to the flag-staff and back again, accomplishing the feat amidst . . . boisterous cheers. . . .

During the next year or two she vibrated between New York and Havana. In most of the oral biographies I have heard, and in one newspaper sketch which I have read, there are vague hints of occasional husbands, nebulous and hazy individuals, who came to the fore briefly and at long intervals, and anon disappeared in the distance, or were dispersed by force of circumstances and condition. There were rumors of . . . married respectability; but nothing of this sort was tangible or ever crystalized into fact. . . . The War of the Rebellion broke out, and in the spring of 1861, with a vast horde of other adventurers, soldiers of fortune, men and women, looking for some lucky chance for fame or fortune, Agnes Leclercq went to Washington.

Thus gossiped Noah Brooks, but never did Agnes satisfy her slanderers. On the contrary, she once wrote:

I am . . . dispensed from the necessity of describing my cradle, the emotions I experienced in admiring my first pair of shoes, and by dissecting my soul for the amusement of some curious people. I confess it affords me a malicious pleasure to disappoint, in this respect, a number of persons who for years have taken the trouble of inventing the most romantic and wonderful stories in reference to my youth, taxing their fancy to the utmost to take revenge on me for my silence.

Agnes was always a woman of spirit and some of it was exhibited in those months in Washington. There, it was actually—but—perhaps—facetiously reported that she had been commissioned a Captain in the volunteer service. In any event, she wore the insignia of that rank, and when, attired in military garb, gilt-buttoned and gold-braided, she rode on Pennsylvania Avenue, followed by a liveried groom, she was a sight to see. A swain declared that "whatever the horse may do, she sits as gracefully and easily in her saddle as if she were sitting before a piano." He had seen her dressed in "very elegant black . . . and a little black hat, with a large scarlet ostrich plume. . . . It was a pleasure to look at her animated sunny face, which was young and pretty. Her complexion was not white and red; but of that mellow light olive tint which we admire in the ladies from the South, and her hair was as black 'as the wing of a raven.' Her smooth forehead was somewhat rounded, and under her finely-penciled arched brows sparkled light-brown eyes, full of mischief and fun. Her fine straight nose was beautifully chiseled, especially at its end, and her nostrils reminded me of those of a fine Arabian horse, though it may not be very polite to indulge in such equine comparisons. Her mouth was rather large; but its full coral lips, and the good natured fun lurking round its corners, made it extremely agreeable and pretty."

As an aside, I beg you to remember those "coral lips." The allusion is not altogether irrelevant.

Agnes knew everybody and went everywhere. One day, when visiting the German Division, on the Virginia side of the Potomac, she met Felix zu Salm-Salm, a Westphalian Princeling and Colonel in a New York Regiment. He had come to America to escape his creditors and had tendered his services to the Union cause. When he had expressed to the President some anxiety lest his hereditary title might prove prejudicial to his progress in a republic, Mr. Lincoln had smilingly replied, "That you are a prince shall be no impediment to your success with us."

When Agnes first beheld him "The Prince was . . . a man of thirty years. He was of middle height, had an elegant figure, dark hair, light mustache, and a very agreeable handsome face, the kind and modest expression of which was highly prepossessing. He had very fine dark eyes, which, however, seemed not to be very good, as he had to use a glass, which he perpetually wore in his right eye, managing it with all the skill of a Prussian officer of the guard."

His demeanor was without "boldness and assurance." Women in general and Agnes in particular found his "bashfulness" irresistible. Eventually she overcame it. Agnes Leclercq and Colonel Felix Salm were married at St. Patrick's Church, Washington, on August 30, 1862. Princess Agnes followed her noble Colonel to the Wars.

In the weeks before Chancellorsville, gaiety had not vanished from the Army of the Potomac, drawn up as it was in fine array at Falmouth. Amenities were many, morale was reasonably sound; hearts were light. Some there were, however, who looked askance at frivolities. One of these was Charles Francis Adams who described the situation there prevailing as "a period in its history when, so far as character was concerned, the Army of the Potomac sank to its lowest point. It was commanded by a trio, of each of whom the least said the better. It consisted of 'Joe' Hooker, 'Dan' Sickles, and 'Dan' Butterfield. All three were men of blemished character. During the winter (1862-63), when Hooker was in command, I can say from personal knowledge and experience, that the Headquarters of the Army of the Potomac was a place to which no self-respecting man liked to go, and no decent woman could go. It was a combination or barroom and brothel."

But such strictures did not destroy the comfort of Colonel Salm and his Princess. They lived in a large hospital tent rendered at once less transparent and more private by doubling and lining it with white and red woolen damask, arranged in festoons, between which flags were fastened. The wooden floor was covered with a carpet. In the living room was a splendid sofa, made by the soldiers. The straw cushions were covered with damask. Salm had, in addition, procured from a neighboring village a large mirror, supposing that his bride could not be happy without it. The Princess Agnes had, however, little occasion to examine herself. Her wardrobe was Spartanly simple: two riding habits, one black, one gray, to provide a change when drenched in the field; and two uniform-like costumes consisting of a petticoat falling to the ankles, and a tight-fitting jacket, both made of cloth.

The bedroom was impressive with a large bedstead, complete with straw mattress, over which was spread a buffalo skin and two blankets. Overhead was a red and white canopy.

They had a tin service for six persons, as well as half a dozen knives and forks. They entertained frequently. Behind what the Princess called her "canvas palace" was a smaller tent, which served as kitchen and dormitory for her maid. A shed was used as stable for the horses.

Food was plentiful. The Salms had their personal ca-

terer and, for wine cellar, a hole was dug in the ground
and filled with bottles of assorted shapes and contents.

At camp the social season was a great success. General
Sickles, still in possession of both legs, acted as *maître-de-
plaisirs*. He gave a party in a hall improvised by combining a dozen or more large hospital tents, decorated inside
and out with flags, garlands, flowers, and Chinese lanterns
in great profusion. The scene was said to be fairy-like.
Supper was laid for two hundred ladies and gentlemen
and the menu could not have been surpassed in Paris.
Presiding over it was Lorenzo Delmonico himself, summoned from New York, and accompanied by staff, silver,
plate, and the choicest delicacies.

Not to be outdone in hospitality, General Birney held
an unforgettable tournament. There were races with and
without hurdles on the drill-ground, wherein, as one participant noticed, "Colonel Prince Salm-Salm came near
breaking his neck. Some of the other officers had fine
tumbles in the mud. But generally these falls were more
comical than dangerous. After returning, there was a
collation at headquarters, we had illuminations, fireworks, and a representation of Negro-minstrels in a theatre put up for that purpose. Nothing was wanting for the
success of the entertainment, at which the whole army
was present."

These festivities and others like them provided the
press with excellent copy and, in consequence, visitors,
eager to live it up, thronged to Falmouth. The news
seems to have penetrated the walls of the Executive Mansion, for it is written of Mary Lincoln that "the thought-
ful wife of the President, an able and a noble woman,
ought to have the credit of originating the plan of a tour

through the Army by the President, as she saw what an excellent effect would be given the troops, now in good condition and ready to march, by coming in contact with their Commander-in-Chief and his family."

The "able and noble woman" seems, as she usually did, to have persuaded her indulgent spouse. In any event, the *Carrie Martin,* a little steamer, left the Washington Navy Yard on the afternoon of April 4, 1863. On board were Mr. and Mrs. Lincoln, their ten-year-old son, Tad, Attorney General Bates, the President's old crony Dr. Anson G. Henry, then Surveyor General of Washington Territory, a Captain Crawford of the Overland Service, and Noah Brooks. It snowed heavily and before nightfall the wind reached gale proportions with the result that the ship put into a cove, opposite Indian Head, where the anchor was dropped until the next morning. It was still snowing when they arrived at Aquia Creek, where a special train, consisting of "a rude freight car, decorated with flags," met the President and his guests and transported them to Falmouth Station.

There the President and his party were met by General Butterfield, Joe Hooker's Chief of Staff accompanied by an escort of lancers, and in carriages they rode "over a fearfully muddy road, 'the sacred soil' red and clayey" to headquarters. For lodgings they were given wall-tents, warmed by stoves and, it was noted, "real sheets" were on the beds. Mr. Lincoln seemed to enjoy the sharp contrast to the White House.

Mr. Lincoln had come for relaxation, but, in the days that followed, he was as fully occupied as ever. Weather permitting, he reviewed the forces, visited hospitals, received callers. He was constantly on horseback and is said

to have exhausted several mounts. When someone remarked that the rest was good for him, he shook his head
dubiously and replied: "I don't know about the 'rest,' as
you call it. I suppose it is good for the body. But the tired
part of me is inside and out of reach."

But once, at least, he was not unpleasantly diverted
from thoughts of war. The episode took place in the early
afternoon of April 7. He had been with the Third Corps
and, as he rode through the lines, General Sickles had
been touched by the sadness that seemed to consume him.
Mr. Lincoln had exclaimed: "Sickles, can you see any end
of this dreadful struggle? It breaks my heart to think of
how many of these brave men, and of how many of their
brave adversaries, will perish before peace can be restored."

Clearly something must be done to relieve the President's depression. Sickles had appointed about one hundred and fifty mounted officers in full uniform to meet
him at his entrance to the camp and escort him to headquarters, where some thirty ladies had assembled to greet
him. One of them was the Princess Agnes and she was
eager. What were her sensations when the President at
last appeared cannot be precisely known, but she later recalled, as she put it, that "his face, beaming with bound-
less kindness and benevolence towards mankind, had the
stamp of intellectual beauty. I could not look into it
without feeling kindly toward him, and without tears
starting to my eyes." She did not, it is true, mention his
coral lips, but she did record "the sly humor flickering
around the corners of his big mouth."

Mr. Lincoln was accompanied only by Tad; Mary Lincoln, suffering from fatigue, had remained behind; other

members of the party had gone off on a sightseeing expedition.

This was the situation when the performance began and it began almost right away. But there are several versions of the preliminaries. Even Dan Sickles, himself an eyewitness, sometimes varied the prologue. Once he gave this explanation: "I noticed that the President was suffering from one of those melancholy moods that sometimes attack men of strong purpose and abundant native wit. After trying in every way that I could to dispel the gloomy thoughts that weighed so heavily upon the President's mind, I at last proposed to the women that they should draw up in line and kiss him. They entered heartily into the joke, but no one seemed equal to the task of being the first. Whereupon I turned to Princess Salm-Salm and declared that as she was the youngest, the spriteliest and the most courageous of the company it should devolve upon her to set the example and head the march.

" 'But, General,' objected the Princess, 'he is so very tall, I will never be able to get up to him.' 'Ah,' replied I, 'if you will but intimate ever so slightly your intention, I am sure Lincoln will do all in his power to overcome the difficulty.'

"It is needless to say," continued the General, "that the idea succeeded. In fact it worked like a charm, and the women were not only amply rewarded for their charming bravery, but the entire camp felt with a renewed force the power and charm concealed in a woman's kiss."

On another occasion General Sickles remembered the story in these terms: "Wishing to turn his thoughts in a cheerful direction, I proposed to several of the ladies present that they should kiss Lincoln, but there were serious objections; none of them were willing to lead off in the charge. One said: 'It is not for us to begin that sort of thing.' Another protested that a woman could not climb up and kiss a man of Lincoln's great height. At last it was agreed that the Princess Salm-Salm, the youthful and attractive wife of the commander of a Union regiment, should give the President the first salute, to be quickly followed by other ladies of the party. Lincoln, it is needless to say, enjoyed the fun; and when I escorted the President back to the headquarters of the Army, I was glad to see that his profound depression, so visible earlier in the morning, had disappeared."

In still another recital, General Sickles supplied dialogue in telling how one of the ladies had come up to him and said: "The President seems to have a very sad look."

"I said: 'Maybe we can do something to make him more cheerful. Suppose you form a line of ladies and each of you give him a kiss.' "

"The proposition did not receive much favor, as there was no one willing to take the lead. I spoke to the Princess Salm-Salm about it, and she agreed to lead off, but she did not see how she could reach the President as he was so very tall—six feet, four."

"I said: 'Maybe the President will meet you halfway; that is I think he will lean down a little.' "

"The Princess Salm-Salm was a charming woman. . . . After I had formed the ladies in line, she went up to him, and sure enough he leaned down a little, and the other ladies followed her example with broad smiles and laughter. After that Lincoln was cheerful."

Now you are well aware of the fact that in these recol-

lections as related by Dan Sickles he claimed for himself
the credit for having considerately originated the idea.
But Julia Butterfield, who got the story directly from her
General-husband, ascribed it to another source. Wrote
Mrs. Butterfield of the incident:

Several ladies belonging to the families of the officers, who
were visiting their husbands before the campaign opened,
were at the Third Corps headquarters. Among them was the
Princess Salm-Salm . . . The Princess, a very beautiful
woman, led the way, and as she approached to be presented to
the President, she said to Sickles, "General, he is a dear, good
man, we want to kiss him; would it do any harm?" "Not a bit
of harm. I am only sorry not to be in his place," was the
gallant reply. A glance from the Princess toward the ladies
following in her train was all that was necessary. They quickly
surrounded Mr. Lincoln, embracing and kissing him with
eagerness and fervor, although it was not easy for them to
reach up . . . If a squadron of cavalry had surrounded the
President and charged right down upon him, he could not
have been more helpless or more confused, yet he smiled and
laughed, and seemed warmly touched by this public expression of hearty, sincere admiration and sympathy.

But Noah Brooks, who often repeated the story of the
bussed-man's holiday, found reason to impugn the mo-
tives of the Princess. He once wrote:

She had met the President before this time, but never so
familiarly as was possible in the unbending of official dignity
during the visit to the army. Anticipating great pleasure from
an opportunity to exercise her power of fascination upon the
good President, she laid a wager of a basket of champagne
with an officer, that she would kiss Mr. Lincoln at a lunch,
which was to be given to the President's party, and General
Hooker, and staff, at Sickles' headquarters . . . And sure

enough, while the company were gravely chatting after lunch, to the astonishment of the good old man [actually he was just turned fifty-four], the audacious Princess suddenly swooped down upon Lincoln, with an exclamation, and, before he could catch his breath, kissed him soundly on the lips. There was a great laugh, and an awkward feeling of suspense; but the President took it so good-humoredly, that another of the ladies rushed up and followed the example just set her, and before the fun was over, every woman in the place had precipitated herself on the hardly-pressed President, each with a bouncing kiss.

In another rendering the impervious, vengeful Brooks altered the forfeit and the scene and relieved the rest of the ladies of complicity and participation in the outrage writing how . . .

This remarkable woman . . . astonished the President, on his entering General Sickle's headquarters, by flying at him, and imprinting a bouncing kiss on his surprised and not altogether attractive face. As soon as he could collect himself and recover from his astonishment, the President thanked the lady, but with evident discomposure; whereupon some of the party made haste to explain that the Princess . . . had laid a wager with one of the officers that she would kiss the President. Her audacious sally won her a pair of gloves.

To the best of my knowledge, the Princess never gave her side of this osculatory impromptu but she may have had it in mind when she wrote in her memoirs that "everything was done by commanding generals to entertain . . . the President."

Alas, her own sublime sacrifice did not long dissipate the Lincoln blues. Little Tad had been a horrified witness to the ceremony and, when it was over, jumped on the bugler's pony and rode back to the wall-tent to tell his mother all about it. That "able and noble woman" went promptly into a mighty rage and, upon Mr. Lincoln's return, berated him with that facility for violence, vituperation, and vindictive vaporing which was her most outstanding quality. At last she demanded to know who the indecorous females had been. When told, she angrily exclaimed: "What could you expect? Those women are all circus riders!" Her excoriations were overheard; news of her noisy tormenting of her lord spread rapidly gathering embellishments along the way. Mrs. Butterfield commented: "if it be true that village gossip runs an express train, it may be said that camp gossip goes by telegraph."

The next morning General Sickles went over to headquarters, but was advised to keep away from Mrs. Lincoln who had been informed that he had been (as he put it) "the one who had suggested the kissing performance."

Poor Sickles! His distressing situation became more acute a day or two later when General Hooker, stupidly or ignorantly or at least incautiously, designated him to accompany the President and his family to the steamer and return with them to Washington. On board the vessel, the President chatted freely, but when they were summoned to dinner Sickles noticed to his grave discomfort that Mrs. Lincoln was "very reserved." Mr. Lincoln did his best to restore her to better temper but to no avail. "She evaded every overture, even the amusing anecdotes he related with characteristic tact and humor. Not a smile softened her stern features."

But at one point the President turned to Sickles, telling him that he had heard, while with the army, that Sickles was "a very pious man."

Sickles replied that if he enjoyed such a reputation he felt confident that he did not deserve it.

Mr. Lincoln insisted, however, that he had learned, from a usually reliable source, that Sickles was "a great Psalmist." Sickles demurred saying that although he had read the Psalms, "as every intelligent person did," he was not "on that account entitled to be known as a pious man or as a Psalmist." He was continuing to protest when the President interrupted him, exclaiming: "Sickles, I have not only heard while in your camp that you are a Psalmist, but I have heard from the best authority that you are a Salm-Salmist."

This bold allusion at once softened Mrs. Lincoln's resentment. She joined in the laugh and offering Sickles her hand, declared amiably that she would let bygones be bygones.

And there the story of the President and the Princess ends. Agnes, of course, went on to further exploits and further glories in Mexico and Europe. She was the heroine of the last days of Maximilian, riding day and night between his prison at Queretaro and the Liberal headquarters, negotiating terms, securing delays in judicial proceedings, and on her knees beseeching Juarez to spare the Emperor's life. For her loyalty to her son, the Archduchess Sophia gave her his miniature set in an emerald bracelet, and the Emperor of Austria conferred on her a pension.

In the Franco-Prussian War she obtained permission from General von Steinmetz—a permission never before granted to a woman—to accompany his staff with the army of invasion, and she exerted herself to the utmost in organizing hospitals and ministering to the wounded.

For her astonishing services she was recommended for honors and decorations.

In 1899 she returned briefly to the United States. A journalist who saw her at New York's Odd Fellows Hall described a part of her costume: "The Princess wore the Grand Cordon, presented to her by the Emperor Maximilian, and the Iron Cross, bestowed by the Prussian government for service in the field, hung beneath the Maximilian medal. On her shoulders were epaulettes." It was during this visit that she was awarded a further distinction. The New York Chapter of the Daughters of the American Revolution elected her an honorary member. Perhaps she added that to her regalia.

It is said that when Felix Constantin Alexander Johann Nepomuk, Prince Salm-Salm, fell bravely at Gravelotte, his thirty-year-old widow, Agnes, betook herself to Rome, there to consult Pope Pius IX concerning her wish to enter a convent. But His Holiness told her firmly that "she had no vocation to be a nun." No one will dispute the infallibility of that decision.

"Act Well Your Part": Being the Story of Mr. Lincoln and the Theater

IT WAS the evening of Good Friday.

The year was 1865.

At the Hub of the Universe, Edwin Booth was appearing in the Boston Theatre as Sir Edward Mortimer in George Colman's play, *The Iron Chest*. He was groaning, "Where is my honour now? Mountains of shame are piled upon me." Recalling those lines, hours later, he would write, "little did I dream . . . that I was not acting but uttering the fearful truth."

At Philadelphia's Walnut Street Theatre, Vestvali the Magnificent was concluding her benefit performance in *Hearts are Trumps* "with a grand display of fireworks." On the morrow, Felicita Vestvali would address a card to the public: "In consequence of the great CALAMITY the Nation has suffered, and my own affliction at the loss of one of my most esteemed friends, I beg to state that I will not be able to perform until Thursday." She was ill.

In Washington, Lieutenant General Grant, for the

third or fourth time, had disappointed an audience by failing to keep a promise to appear.

At Grover's New Theatre, on Pennsylvania Avenue near Willard's, Master Thomas Lincoln and his tutor had been seated in the front to see the great oriental spectacle, *Aladdin! or, the Wonderful Lamp.* There they watched the surprising mechanical effects, the grand ballets and tableaux, and listened to the beautiful music rendered by Mr. Koppitz and his company. An usher touched Tad on the shoulder, bidding him to return at once to the Executive Mansion.

At Ford's, a few blocks away, the bearded man in an overcoat had fallen from the rocking chair to the floor of his box; his bleeding head lay in the lap of lovely Laura Keene.

A crazed and crippled player on horseback rode toward Maryland.

The story of Lincoln's murder is known to everyone; the theater and its people are inseparable from it. But strangely: the influence of the theater and its people upon his life has received only the most casual consideration of his biographers. This is the more surprising because they have been content to recognize the attraction, the affinity and—to let it go at that. Thus Carl Sandburg has written that Mr. Lincoln was himself "a practiced actor and an individual artist in the use of his face . . . He had grown up in a society where the theatre and professional dramatic entertainments were scarce, and in the idle evenings and on rainy days people had to create art by themselves." Again, in the final volume of Professor James G. Randall's *Lincoln the President,* there is risked

this surmise: "Doubtless he would have made a powerful tragic actor as well as a discerning drama critic."

But there is contemporary evidence to support a feeling that Mr. Lincoln was not himself completely unaware
of his faculty for histrionics. On the night of March 2,
1864, the painter, Francis Carpenter, was at the White
House, working on his picture, the reading of the Eman-
cipation Proclamation, and listening intently as the President recited the opening lines of Richard III. Of that
experience Mr. Carpenter has left this record: "I could
not refrain from laying down my palette and brushes,
and applauding heartily, upon his conclusion, saying, at
the same time, half in earnest, that I was not sure but that
he had made a mistake in the choice of a profession, considerably, as may be imagined, to his amusement." Perhaps, there must be a bit of "ham" in all our public men;
certainly Abraham Lincoln was not always immune to it.

But it is necessary to inquire, when was Mr. Lincoln's
interest in the drama first aroused and how was it sustained? A competent student (the late F. Lauriston Bul-
lard) has guessed that it may well have begun with a visit
to the American Theatre in New Orleans, when he journeyed to the shining city on a flatboat, when he was in
his early twenties and when all the world was new. However that may be, it *is* known that, while a resident of New
Salem, he consumed such of the writings of the illustrious
prodigy of Stratford as he could lay his hands on and, with
less avidity, the writings of some of the lesser playwrights.

In any event, it would seem to be safe to say that, up
to the time of his removal to Springfield, his knowledge
of the theater was largely academic or vicarious. But
shortly thereafter something happened: the Illinois The-

atrical Company came to town, resolved "to devote the
entire season to the entertainment of the members of the
legislature." First, however, it was necessary to erect a
playhouse, "the timber of which was taken from the
woods and worked into a theatre in ten days." It was
ninety feet deep, forty feet wide and wholly without or-
namentation of any kind. Nevertheless, the proprietors
who had never "owned anything with a roof until now
. . . were naturally proud of their possession." At last
all was in readiness.

But, simultaneously with the construction, a successful
religious revival had been in progress and among the con-
verts were those who held that piety and players were
inherently incompatible. Joseph Jefferson, then a little
boy, who accompanied his father, a proprietor of the
company, later reported the ensuing crisis in these words:

The fathers of the church not only launched forth against
us in their sermons, but by some political manoeuver got the
city to pass a new law enjoining a heavy license against our
"unholy" calling; I forget the amount, but it was large
enough to be prohibitory. Here was a terrible condition of
affairs: all our available funds invested, the legislature in ses-
sion, the town full of people, and we by a heavy license denied
the privilege of opening the new theater.

In the midst of their troubles a young lawyer called on the
managers. He had heard of the injustice, and offered, if they
would place the matter in his hands, to have the license taken
off, declaring that he only desired to see fair play, and he
would accept no fee whether he failed or succeeded. The case
was brought up before the council. The young lawyer began
his harangue. He handled the subject with tact, skill, and
humor, tracing the history of the drama from the time when
Thespis acted in a cart, to the stage of the day. He illustrated

his speech with a number of anecdotes, and kept the council in a roar of laughter; his good-humor prevailed, and the exorbitant tax was taken off.

And Mr. Jefferson added:

The young lawyer was very popular in Springfield, and was honored and beloved by all who knew him, and after the time of which I write he held rather an important position in the Government of the United States. He now lies buried near Springfield, under a monument commemorating his greatness and his virtues—and his name was Abraham Lincoln!

'Tis a pleasant tale, but distressingly tainted with improbability. One formidable authority, conceding that it "has become firmly imbedded in the folklore of Illinois," has dismissed it as apocryphal on the ground that "the minutes of the town council show that Lincoln was not present when the case was considered." Another scholar has taken a more lenient view, arguing that the failure to record Mr. Lincoln's name "does not necessarily rule out the possibility of his having appeared on behalf of the players," and observing that "appearances may not have been noted so scrupulously in those days." Certainly the account is neither implausible, nor out of character, but until contemporary evidence is found to sustain it, dubiety will persist.

Be that as it may, there is sound reason to suppose that in the years that followed (and particularly after his marriage to the tense Miss Todd), Abraham Lincoln made the most of infrequent opportunities for distraction. It was sometime in 1857 that a lady-elocutionist descended on the seat of Sangamon County and gave a public reading in a hall immediately north of the State House. There she rendered, with some emotion, Butler's *Nothing to Wear;* what transpired is thus related by an eyewitness:

In the midst of one stanza, in which no effort is made to say anything particularly amusing, and during the reading of which the audience manifested the most respectful silence and attention, some one in the rear seats burst into a loud, coarse laugh—a sudden and explosive guffaw. It startled the speaker and audience, and kindled a storm of unsuppressed laughter and applause. Everyone looked back to ascertain the cause of the demonstration, and was greatly surprised to find that it was Mr. Lincoln. He blushed and squirmed with the awkward diffidence of a schoolboy. What prompted him to laugh no one was able to explain. He was doubtless wrapped up in a brown study, and, recalling some amusing episode, indulged in laughter without realizing his surroundings. The experience mortified him greatly.

Another unforgettable evening was the evening of March 23, 1860. The Chicago Convention in the Wigwam was only a few weeks away. Mr. Lincoln was a candidate for the Presidential nomination. With his old friend, Henry Clay Whitney, he attended the performance of Rumsey & Newcomb's Minstrels. Of his behavior on that occasion, Mr. Whitney has left this account:

The nondescript song and dance of *Dixie* was sung and acted by this troupe, the first time I ever saw it, and probably the first time it was sung and acted in Illinois. I can remember well the spontaneity of Mr. Lincoln's enthusiasm, and the heartiness of his applause at the music and action of this rollicking and eccentric performance. . . . He clapped his great brawny hands in true rustic heartiness and exclaimed in riotous enthusiasm: "Let's have it again! Let's have it again."

Parenthetically, it may be noted that, for Mr. Lincoln, this favorable impression was enduring. A week before his death, when he was on the *River Queen,* at City Point, the Headquarters Band came aboard and offered to play request numbers. Turning to the Marquis de Chambrun, who stood beside him, Mr. Lincoln asked if he had ever heard the rebel song, "Dixie," to the sound of which all the Southern attacks had been conducted. The reply was in the negative; whereupon the President remarked: "That tune is now Federal property and it is good to show the rebels that, with us in power, they will be free to hear it again," and he told the surprised musicians to play it which they did with spirit and delight.

Throughout the War years, Mr. Lincoln was in constant touch with members of the theatrical profession. Miss Charlotte Cushman, who has been called "the most powerful actress America has produced," waited upon him in the early summer of 1861, and was treated, as she put it, with "great courtesy & marked respect." Mr. Lincoln must have been in rare form on that occasion, for, several days later, she wrote to her good friend, William H. Seward, the Secretary of State:

At the risk of seeming a bore I thrust myself again on your valuable time, begging you to forgive me. I have to thank you for so much pleasure & comfort in my short sojourn near you, that I ought to be ashamed to ask anything more of you, & for myself I would not—I took the liberty of speaking to you about my young friend in whom I took much interest, whom I wished to have placed at West Point Military Academy. You advised my asking the President when, if I found him in a "pliant hour" you would take care to keep the young man in your mind. When you did me the honor to present me, I was so completely taken up with him & his humor that I forgot my mission & came away.

Another example is found in a letter written to the President by a prominent impresario, at Bridgeport, Connecticut, August 30, 1861:

Honored Sir,
The late events which have occurred in this vicinity, concluding with the arrest of *Schnabel,* have rendered secessionists *so scarce* I cannot find one for exhibition in my museum.

Those who one week ago were blatant secessionists, are to day publicly announcing themselves as "in for the country to the end of the war." The "strong arm" has a mighty influence here.

It was signed: "Phineas T. Barnum."
People from the theater were always welcome at the Executive Mansion, among them were James E. Murdoch, who gave Shakespearean readings, John E. McDonough, with whom Mr. Lincoln discussed *Henry IV;* and Mr. Hermann, the magician, who "performed some of his wonderful feats" for the mystification of His Excellency and consort. But what was, perhaps, the most unusual ceremony was held on the day following Mr. Lincoln's fifty-fourth birthday. Grace Greenwood, who was present, has recounted it in these terms:

During a visit to Washington . . . I received an informal invitation to a reception *extraordinaire* at the White House. It was to meet Mr. and Mrs. Charles Stratton—"General Tom Thumb"—and his wife Lavinia, then on their bridal tour. . . . The reception took place in the East Room; and when, following the loud announcement, "Mr. and Mrs. Charles Stratton," the guests of honor entered from the corridor, and

walked slowly up the long *salon,* to where Mr. and Mrs.
Lincoln stood, to welcome them, the scene became interesting
tho' a little bizarre. The pigmy "General," at that time still
rather good looking, tho' slightly *blasé,* wore his elegant wedding suit, and his wife, a plump but symmetrical little woman,
with a bright intelligent face, her wedding dress—the regula-
tion white satin, with point lace, orange blossoms and pearls
—while a train some two yards long swept out behind her.
I well remember the "pigeon-like stateliness," with which
they advanced, almost to the feet of the President, and the
profound respect with which they looked up, up, to his kindly
face. It was pleasant to see their tall host bend, and bend, to
take their little hands in his great palm, holding Madame's
with especial chariness, as tho' it were a robin's egg, and he
were fearful of breaking it. Yet he did not *talk* down to them,
but made them feel from the first as tho' he regarded them as
real "folks," sensible, and knowing a good deal of the world.
He presented them very courteously and soberly, to Mrs.
Lincoln, and in his compliments and congratulations there
was not the slightest touch of the exaggeration which a lesser
man might have been tempted to make use of, for the quiet
amusement of on-lookers; in fact, nothing to reveal to that
shrewd little pair his keen sense of the incongruity of the
scene.

By way of a wedding present, Mr. and Mrs. Lincoln
gave Mr. and Mrs. Stratton "a gorgeous set of Chinese
fire screens."

Indeed, the Lincolns were, throughout their Washington residence, a stage-struck family. Tad, for example,
converted one of the vacant rooms of the White House
into a miniature theater, complete with stage, curtains,
orchestra pit, parquet and other appropriate parapher-
nalia. But in their first months, the Lincolns had little
opportunity fully to gratify their passion. For this denial

there were two explanations. The first derived from the fact that the old Washington Theatre, on Eleventh Street near C, was the only place in town given over to the "legitimate drama." It was small, uncomfortable, and conspicuous for indifferent productions. The second was caused by Willie Lincoln's death in February, 1862, which plunged the family into harrowing grief and heavy mourning.

In the following month, John Thomson Ford opened the Washington Athenaeum, described as a "splendid establishment," on Tenth Street near E, in the premises lately occupied by the First Baptist Church. (That Washington's religious structures are readily adaptable to entertainment was again demonstrated in the early nineteen twenties when St. Mark's Church on Fifteenth Street became, by minor transformation, the Cafe St. Mark's.) In any event, Ford's Washington Athenaeum flourished for a few months, until half-past five in the afternoon of Tuesday, December 30, when it was "entirely consumed by fire." It was promptly rebuilt and on Thursday evening, August 27, 1863, it was thrown open to the public, with "a tremendous crowd . . . in attendance."

Meanwhile, on April 22, 1862, the New National Theatre, on Pennsylvania Avenue, near Willard's popular hotel, had opened. The old National, incidentally, had been destroyed by fire, soon after Mr. Buchanan's inauguration, at a time when the unfortunate Mr. Ford was the lessee. Now the *New* National was solemnly dedicated as a "Temple of the Muses" and of its new tenant, Mr. Leonard Grover, it was written that he "has thus far surpassed the attempts of any other manager to establish a popular and refined public resort; and, having every confidence in his ability and experience, we feel sure of his eventual success."

Thereafter, Mr. Lincoln became a steady and consistent playgoer. With respect to his attendance, Mr. Grover once wrote that . . .

He visited my theater probably more than a hundred times. He often came alone, many times brought his little son Tad, and on special occasions, Mrs. Lincoln. It was evident that Mr. Lincoln came to be alone. At times he invited me to sit in the box with him, when such conversation as took place was always about the theater. As auditor, or spectator, Mr. Lincoln was not exacting. As is well known, he was exceedingly conversant with Shakespeare. He enjoyed a classical representation, of which I gave a great many.

Colonel John W. Forney, who called himself the "Editor of the Organ of the Republican Party," wrote:

Mr. Lincoln liked the theatre not so much for itself as because of the rest it afforded him. I have seen him more than once looking at a play without seeming to know what was going on before him. Abstracted and silent, scene after scene would pass, and nothing roused him until some broad joke or curious antic disturbed his equanimity.

This view was confirmed by the President's intimate and confidant, Noah Brooks, who once declared:

He went often to the theatre, usually accompanied only by a friend and taking great pains to enter the place unrecognized. He sought the theatre only as a means of amusing a spare hour, diverting his mind from the cares and sorrows that weighed him down.

At another time, Brooks testified that Mr. Lincoln "was on such terms with the managers of two of the theaters that he could go in privately by the stage door, and slip into the stage boxes without being seen by the audience. Concealed by the friendly screen of the drapery, he saw many plays without public observation."

And at still another time Brooks recalled:

It was Mr. Lincoln's delight to sally forth in the darkness, on foot, and, accompanied only by a friend, to visit some theater to which notice of his coming had been sent only just before his setting out. When we consider that it was popularly believed that Washington at that time was infested with spies and midnight assassins, we may well wonder at his temerity. But perhaps it was the unexpectedness and lack of advertisement of his movements that may have induced him to undertake these little excursions. It was the wide publicity given to his intention to go to the play that wrought his own undoing in 1865.

These expeditions, essentially incognito, were a source of grave concern and severe distress to the President's responsible guardians. Thus at half-past one on the morning of December 10, 1864, the Marshal of the District of Columbia, Colonel Ward Hill Lamon, felt obliged to indite this indignant protest:

To-night as you have done on several previous occasions, you went unattended to the theatre. When I say unattended, I mean that you went alone with Charles Sumner and a foreign minister, neither of whom could defend himself against as assault from any able-bodied woman in the city. And you know, or ought to know, that your life is sought after, and will be taken unless you and your friends are cautious; for you have many enemies within our lines.

But despite his clandestine entrances and exits, Mr. Lincoln was not, in the modern sense, a stage-door Johnnie. Leonard Grover's partner, Colonel William E. Sinn, to whom we owe the information that Mr. Lincoln cared little for vaudeville, and visited Canterbury Hall, the variety house, "only once or twice," is the author of the statement that—

One peculiar feature about Mr. Lincoln's theater going was that he never had the least desire (as many theatergoers have) to go behind the scenes. He used to say that to do so would spoil the illusion surrounding the play. When very prominent actors appeared, however, in whom he was specially interested, Mr. Lincoln would invite them into his private box between the acts, and have a chat with them. He was a great admirer of the drama, and was particularly fond of comedy.

On March 13, 1863, Mr. Lincoln paid "a spontaneous visit to the Washington theatre." It had been refurbished and was then under the management of John T. Raymond. It was then Mr. Lincoln's habit to go down there at night, sit in the manager's office for an hour and chat, and then pass through the stage door unnoticed to his private box. The play that evening was *Henry IV;* the Falstaff, James H. Hackett. Mr. Hackett was flattered to learn of this mark of magisterial favor and, upon his return to New York a few days later he sent the President a copy of his *Notes and Comments Upon Certain Plays and Actors of Shakespeare,* which had recently issued from the press.

Mr. Lincoln had other things on his mind and did not get around to expressing his pleasure in the gift until August 17; on that day he wrote:

Months ago I should have acknowledged the receipt of your book, and accompanying kind note; and I now have to beg your pardon for not having done so.

For one of my age, I have seen very little of the drama. The first presentation of Falstaff I ever saw was yours here last winter or spring. Perhaps the best compliment I can pay is to say, as I truly can, I am very anxious to see it again. Some of Shakespeare's plays I have never read; while others, I have gone over perhaps as frequently as any unprofessional reader. Among the latter are Lear, Richard Third, Henry Eighth, Hamlet, and especially Macbeth. I think nothing equals Macbeth. It is wonderful. Unlike you gentlemen of the profession, I think the soliloquy in Hamlet commencing "O, my offence is rank" surpasses that commencing "To be, or not to be." But pardon this small attempt at criticism. I should like to hear you pronounce the opening speech of Richard the Third. Will you not soon visit Washington again? If you do, please call and let me make your personal acquaintance.

Mr. Hackett was notoriously a name-dropper. He gloried in his acquaintance with the well-placed and the powerful. Upon receiving Mr. Lincoln's apologia, he issued it as a broadside, under the title, "A Letter from President Lincoln to Mr. Hackett," and with the notice: "Printed not for publication but for private distribution only, and its convenient perusal by personal friends."

Inevitably, copies were made available to the press; its contents were seized upon by political enemies, and there followed a storm of derisive editorial invective directed against the illiterate yokel who presumed to express his untutored preferences. The furore left Mr. Hackett strangely unabashed; he blithely informed the President:

About a month since my son John K. Hackett of New York wrote to me how vexed he had been at the unwarrantable liberty taken by certain Newspaper Presses in publishing your kind, sensible & unpretending letter to me of "17 Aug't" last & more particularly at the Editorial remarks upon & perversion of its subject-matter to antagonistic political purposes, accompanied by satirical abuse in general.

In order to calm my son's fears that it might give you cause to regret your having thus favored me with such original material, I replied that I felt assured that as a man of the world now and an experienced politician you were not likely to be so thin skinned, and that in my humble opinion such political squibs would probably affect your sensibilities about as much as would a charge of mustard seed shot at forty yards distance fired through a pop-gun barrel at the naturally armed Alligator touch his nerves—pray excuse the illustration! But my son being a first rate shot with gun or pistol & thoroughly aware of their comparative effects, it was therefore an *argumentum ad hominen.*

I have just rec'd from my son the enclosed cut from the N. Y. Herald of 16th inst., transcribing an Editorial from "The Liverpool (Eng.) Post of October 1st."

The enclosed editorial was long; it dealt with the letter to Hackett; its object was not unfriendly. And yet it contained some statements which are curious and startling in the perspective of history; it began:

Perhaps no leader in a great contest ever stood so little chance of being a subject of hero worship as Abraham Lincoln, the President of the United States. . . . Every visitor that goes to Washington has something disrespectful to say of his very long legs and consequently very long pantaloons; of his shambling figure; of his awkward speech and doubly awkward silence; of his general unfitness in appearance and manners to mix in high society. Those who only know him from his exercitations in print conceive a but little better opinion of him. His grammar is decidedly self taught and perhaps not quite remembered; his style is no style at all; his arguments seem sometimes to have been written rather on the principle of Samson making sport of the Philistines than as at all adapted to advance his cause; and some of his metaphors are voted decidely below par *by the crowd of arrogant pretenders* to taste who never admired a saying that was tinged with vulgarity, *and never said one that could be suspected of vigor and originality.*

Here these excerpts are interrupted to remark that six weeks after their publication, Mr. Lincoln would go to Gettysburg where he would dedicate the cemetery of the fallen with an address which some consider eligible for admission to literature.

The Liverpool commentary continued to expatiate upon Mr. Lincoln's uncouth propensities but when it had exhausted them, the tone changed:

Yet a worshipper of human heroes might travel a great deal farther and fare much worse for an idol than in selecting this same lanky American—the personification of free soil principles—the representative of the idea that slavery, without being interfered with, must not be allowed to spread itself over the North American continent—and the impersonation, also, of the victory of that idea—a victory, which, as it were, stands on the defensive against those who would turn it into defeat.

As to the Hackett letter, the *Post* insisted that it—

. . . speaks for itself as favorably as any letter ever spoke. Its simplicity and candor are as fresh and delightful as new mown hay. *Only fancy a statesman, a President, confessing thus frankly he has never read Shakespeare through. How many British M. P.'s would have confessed it?* And yet how many of them there are who would have to own as much if they were put to it. . . . The choice of 'Macbeth' as principal favorite, and the preference of the less popular of Hamlet's soliloquies, also indicate the incisive use of his own wits which is one of the surest indications of a man of power.

The *Post* concluded by saying that "Mr. Lincoln . . . is a man whose simple truth and cultivated intelligence will not forever be concealed by the unwieldiness of his frame or the uncourtliness of his manners. *A contrast was wanted to the suave deceitfulness and emptiness of James Buchanan, and one was found in Abraham Lincoln."*

This enclosure must have brought comfort and reassurance to Mr. Lincoln. Replying to Hackett, he told him of the "pleasure" with which he looked forward to the fulfillment of a promised visit and then, getting to the point, wrote:

Give yourself no uneasiness on the subject mentioned . . .

My note to you I certainly did not expect to see in print; yet I have not been much shocked by the newspaper comments upon it. Those comments constitute a fair specimen of what has occurred to me through life. I have endured a great deal of ridicule without much malice; and I have received a great deal of kindness, not quite free from ridicule. I am used to it.

There is every indication that Mr. Lincoln enjoyed his relations with Hackett. John Hay, writing in his diary on December 13, 1863, noted, "Tonight Hackett arrived and spent the evening with the President. The conversation at first took a professional turn, the Tycoon showing a very intimate knowledge of those plays of Shakespeare where Falstaff figures. . . . Hackett is a very amusing and

garrulous talker." On the next evening Mr. Lincoln went
to see Hackett's performance at Ford's Theatre, on the
following evening he returned, and on the seventeenth he
was back again. Early in 1864, at Hackett's request, Mr.
Lincoln secured the discharge of one Oscar Decatur Hall,
of the Fourth U. S. Artillery, whose sister had married Hackett's son. In August of that year, Mr. Hackett
blandly announced to the President:

As an episode, let me mention that, after having been a
widower upwards of 18 years, & reached the age of *64*, &
supposed by many to have acquired with my knowledge of
the world more discretion, I have recently married again,
"achieved a maid"—not that "paragons description & wild
fame," but an unsophisticated country girl, of 25, of *Northern*
New York whose father was a farmer & a *neighbor* when I
resided at *Utica* forty years ago. Some, however, *think* of me,
as Sir Edward Mortimer did of Adam Winterton, in the play
of *The Iron Chest*—"a young and sturdy evergreen that
smiles in the midst of blast and desolation whilst all around
him withers" but I know, of myself, that I have not yet begun
to feel any of the physical infirmities common to men at my
years, & as Sir Pertinax said, *when he had run away with his
second wife from boarding school,* "I am ready to begin the
world again."

His achievement of a maid (who was soon a matron)
and his readiness to start life anew, made Mr. Hackett
wish to retire from the stage and embark upon another
career. He let Mr. Lincoln know that he would accept
a diplomatic post. He at first aspired to be Secretary of
Legation at the Court of St. James's, but when that pros-
pect dimmed he contented himself by seeking to become
Consul General, at London. He told the President how—

The late *Davy Crockett* contended with his fellow Member of Congress, the late C. C. Cambrelling, in palliation of the charge which he admitted he could not entirely deny—"want of edication"—that "some men were too high larnt—John Quincy Adams being one of such, his superfluous larning sometimes confused his head and his purpose."

A comparable affliction befell Mr. Hackett. His head and his purpose became confused. In his quest for patronage, he went too far. He rounded up thirty gentlemen including Cornelius Vanderbilt, William B. Astor, Simeon Draper, Senator Edwin D. Morgan, an ex-Governor of New York, the Vice President of the State Chamber of Commerce, sundry shipowners, bankers, merchants, and "other eminent . . . & influential" personages to subscribe their names to a petition presenting "for your Excellency's favorable consideration their esteemed and respected fellow-citizen, James H. Hackett, as a suitable person to fill the U. S. Consulate at London." Mr. Hackett was persistent; he came to Washington to press his claims. On Saturday night, January 7, 1865, he wrote forlornly to Mr. Lincoln from his room at Willard's:

I did purpose to return to-day to New York, but, having for the last three days inquired & found no opportunity to present myself & my respects to you, & remembering your observation last winter that *Sunday* evenings were the only ones when you would be sure of your ability to receive social calls from your friends, I have resolved to stop here until Monday & venture to drop in upon you about 8 o'clock tomorrow evening.

Apparently Hackett carried out his siege, for Noah Brooks has written of—

. . . going to the President's cabinet on a summons from him very late at night [when] I noticed this man [Hackett] waiting alone in the corridor outside the President's door. Lincoln asked me if anyone was waiting without, and when I told him that I had seen the actor sitting there, he made a gesture of impatience and regret, and said that the little courtesies which had passed between them had resulted in the comedian applying to him for an office. I have forgotten what it was, but I think it was an English consulate which the old man wanted. Lincoln almost groaned as he said that it seemed impossible for him to have any close relations with people in Washington without finding that the acquaintance thus formed generally ended with an application for office.

The curtain had fallen on the *affaire* Hackett, but for Mr. Lincoln whose confession of unfamiliarity with the theater had received so much and such adverse publicity, the experience had one marked affect: he determined to make up his lost time. He went oftener and more publicly to the theater and some of the performances he attended are variously endowed with piquancy or poignancy.

A statement contained in Alexander Hunter's *New National Theater, Washington, D. C.: a Record of Fifty Years,* published in 1885, has found its way into the literature of the conspiracy:

On Saturday, April 11, 1863, the announcement is made that the distinguished young actor, John Wilkes Booth, will make his first appearance in Washington as "King Richard the III."

A very large and fashionable audience greeted him, and, a singular coincidence, President Lincoln and Senator Oliver P. Morton occupied a private box. As the great Lincoln sat there, heartily applauding the young actor, how little he imagined that he beheld his fate, and the delicate hand that handed the signet ring in play to the Governor of the tower, was destined to hold the fatal weapon that was destined to end his own life at a time when he had climbed the very pinnacle of human greatness.

It may be said of this excited report, as Mr. Lincoln once said in another connection: "No harm, if true, but, in fact, not true." Oliver Perry Morton was not, at that time, a United States Senator. He was Governor of Indiana. As for Abraham Lincoln: he had returned late the night before from a "holiday" with Joe Hooker's Army, then still intact at Falmouth. On the night of April 11 he did, it is true, attend the theater; it was not, however, Grover's National, but the Washington, where he laughed with delight at the farcial behavior of Mrs. John Wood in the rôle of Pocahontas. If he saw Booth on another occasion during that engagement, it is not of record.

But it *is* known that on Monday, April 13, 1863, Booth paid the first of several visits to a Washington physician, Dr. John Frederick May, who treated him for a fibroid tumor on his neck. Booth, for reasons of his own, enjoined the doctor "to say, (if questioned upon the fact of his having undergone a surgical operation), that it was for the removal of a bullet." This recalls the singular fact that, like Mr. Lincoln, Booth had once been shot while in a theater. The location of the wound presents a tantalizing, if somewhat amusing, mystery, for the reason that it has been assigned to at least three parts of his anatomy. According to one version, which places Booth in Columbus, Georgia:

The night he was to play Hamlet another actor was with him [Booth] in his dressing room when Canning entered and jokingly threatened to shoot both of them. The gun unexpectedly exploded and Wilkes "was shot in the rear." This accident kept him off the stage for several weeks.

According to another rendering: "While acting," in Montgomery, Alabama, "Wilkes, becoming involved in a quarrel on one occasion, was shot in the neck." But what gives the incident a special singularity is the statement that "the ball remained imbedded in the flesh for a period of perhaps two years, and came out unexpectedly during his first engagement at Grover's Theater, in the spring of 1863." What if Mr. Lincoln had been a witness to that extraordinary extrusion!

By all accounts the man who pulled the trigger was Booth's one-time manager, Matthew W. Canning, "a man about 5 feet 9 inches in height, pale countenance, hair brown, very thin, with moustache and goatee." He was once described as "an exploded Philadelphia lawyer, who took to managing by passing the bar." When he was arrested, at his Camden, New Jersey home, on Saturday night, April 15, 1865, there was found on his person the manuscript of a "brief biography of J. Wilkes Booth." It contained still another variation: "In the season of 1859, he [Booth] made his first appearance as a Star in Columbus, Ga., the Theatre there being under the management of a gentleman from this City [Philadelphia], who during the first week of his engagement, accidentally shot Booth in the side: After his recovery he made his appearance under the same management in Montgomery, Ala., where he played a highly successful engagement."

In the autumn of 1863, Leonard Grover invited the President to inaugurate the new season, by accepting "a double box with connecting door," for a presentation of *Othello,* with James W. Wallack and Edward L. Davenport "in parts of nearly equal strength." Mr. Grover's choice for the day of opening was October 5, but he hastened to add, "Should the date . . . conflict with any different arrangement your Excellency may have in view, I will gladly with your permission postpone the day of opening one or two days to have the gratification of your presence." Accordingly, the production was delayed for twenty-four hours, when the reporter of the *Morning Chronicle* "noticed in the private boxes the President of the United States and members of his cabinet, with their families, and scattered through the parquette and dress circles many of the most distinguished citizens of Washington."

A fortnight thereafter, the National was given over to a performance of *Macbeth* for the benefit of the United States Sanitary Commission which executed some of the present functions of the U.S.O. Charlotte Cushman, who usually played male rôles, on this occasion took the part of Lady Macbeth; she was supported by Messrs. Wallack and Davenport. Financially it was a resounding success, netting more than two thousand dollars. Mr. and Mrs. Lincoln, Tad, and a secretary, William O. Stoddard, "occupied the lower stage boxes to the right, and Secretary Seward, Lord Lyons, and others of note, those opposite."

Three days later, the President and Mrs. Lincoln went to see the fascinating Maggie Mitchell in *Fanchon, the Cricket,* and on November 9, Mr. and Mrs. Lincoln, with a small party, watched the performance of John Wilkes Booth who was playing in *The Marble Heart,* by Dumas. John Hay, who had accompanied the Presidential couple, described the show in his diary as "Rather tame than otherwise." The President's reaction has not been ascertained, but the following paragraph found in the Philadelphia *Press* for April 20, 1865, may refer to that evening:

The personal relations existing before the murder between Booth and the President, augment the horror of the occurrence. Mr. Lincoln saw Booth play more than once, and particularly admired him. He once applauded him rapturously, and with all that genial heartiness for which he was distinguished. Booth, when told of the President's delight, said to his informant that he would rather have the applause of a negro. The President had never spoken with Booth, but wished to make his acquaintance. Booth evaded the interview.

On Tuesday evening, January 19, 1864, Mr. Grover presented "the most beautiful of modern dramas," *The Ticket-of Leave Man,* where, "attracted by this enchanting play," President and Mrs. Lincoln were present.

Following this engagement came the capture of Washington—not by Lee's forces, but by the irresistible Vestvali. Her invasion has been strangely overlooked by Mr. Lincoln's usually diligent and grubbing biographers. Indeed, they mention her not at all. It is high time to restore her to her tantalizing place.

Born Anna Marie Stegemann, as some say, at Stettin in 1829, as others insist, at Warsaw in 1831, her mother was the Baroness Von Hunefold, her father a Polish Count who held the rank of General in the Prussian Army. According to Francois Fétis, "the young girl, who was endowed with a majestic physique and an opulent beauty, had a taste for the arts." At an early age, she made her dramatic debut in Berlin, achieved success, and then, having discovered that she possessed a superb contralto voice, she resolved to cultivate it by taking lessons in Italy from Mercadante and Pietro Romani. When she had finished her musical education, she was engaged at Milan's La Scala, adopted the name of Felicita Vestvali, and there, in 1853, in the role of d'Azucena in *Trovatore,* she won a threefold triumph as woman, as actress, and as singer. This was followed by a brilliant engagement in London and, soon after, she left for New York, where, on February 13, 1855, at Tripler Hall, she sang the part of Arsace in the Grisi and Mario production of *Semiramide,* under the management of Mr. Lincoln's future friend, James H. Hackett.

After a short appearance at the Paris Opéra in 1859, she returned to America. At the time of her Washington advent, early in 1864, she was at the height of her powers. A local paper declared:

Mlle. Vestvali has long sustained the reputation of [being] one of the greatest of lyrical tragic artistes, and her recent brilliant success at Niblo's Garden, New York, New Chestnut Street Theatre, Philadelphia, and in the cities of Louisville, Pittsburg, &c., where she has been playing to houses crowded to excess (hundreds being turned from the door nightly, unable to obtain admission) has stamped her as one of the greatest actresses of the age.

On Thursday, January 28, 1864, she appeared, at the National, in *Gamea, or, the Jewish Mother.* This play had been first produced in Paris, three years before, where it ran for nine consecutive months. Its authorship was ascribed to Victor Séjour, but it was well understood actually to be the work of Monsieur Mocquard, Secretary to the Third Napoleon. Its popularity derived, in part, from its bearing upon the case of Edgar Mortara, a Jewish boy who, in 1858 (the year of the Lincoln-Douglas Debates), had been forcibly removed from his parents on orders from the Archbishop of Bologna. This had led to protests from several powers, but the Pope had declined to interfere. For an American audience, the play had been adapted by Matilda Heron, with music composed by Miss Heron's husband, Robert Stoepel. On this occasion the President and family were present and it was said that "the performance went off with the greatest éclat." The Lincolns were impressed; they reappeared the following evening. The *Chronicle*'s doting reporter wrote:

Grover's [National] Theatre was crowded again . . . by a large and most enthusiastic audience to witness the charming Vestvali in her great impersonation of Allessandro Massaroni, in the musical drama of "The Brigands." Mlle. Vestvali created a profound sensation in the character of the *Brigand.* Her singing of the different songs of the play created a perfect *furore.* . . .
President Lincoln and family again were present . . . Indeed, our worthy President seems as much charmed with the *"Magnificent Vestvali"* as the balance of mankind.

The paper for February 3 announced that the play selected from her repertory for that evening would be *The Duke's Motto,* and continued:

That Vestvali will create excitement in the part, none can doubt. Her magnificent form will show to full advantage in the different costumes of the drama—while that glorious *abandon* which she can impart to a role of this character will all combine to make the performance not only great but a sensational one.

It was. A reviewer announced:

"The Duke's Motto" was produced last evening . . . to a very large and fashionable audience. President Lincoln and wife were present, occupying private boxes.

"The Duke's Motto" is a translation and adaptation by Mr. John Brougham of Paul Féval's play, *"Le Bassu,"* which created a furore at the Porte St. Martin Theatre, Paris. The characters do nothing because it is natural, probable, or even possible, but everything because it is striking, romantic, or will look well from the front, no matter whether it may be unnatural, impassable, or simply and absolutely impossible. The result is a most striking play, crowded full of the most exciting and interesting incidents, and unsurpassed in picturesque and effective situations. . . . We can find no words of praise too extreme for Mlle. Vestvali's acting when she disguised herself as *Esop, the Hunchback;* the audience was completely deceived, and shouts of astonishment and delight greeted her resumption of her original dress and manner.

Was this lady-environed-in-glamour invited to the Presidential box? Was she received at the Executive Mansion? Or did she in some other way make Mr. Lincoln's personal acquaintance? There are no facts from which to form an answer. But it seems very probable that Mr. Lincoln extended her some mark of consideration. To begin with, her gifts obviously pleased him and he was not one to overlook an opportunity for gentle gallantry. Then, too, there is the fact that he was never quite unaffected by a pretty face. But most significantly of all, there is the reference in her card to the public, at the moment of Mr. Lincoln's death, to "my own affliction at the loss of one of my most esteemed friends."

But it must be admitted that there were other reasons why she might have grieved at his passing. She was, at that time, playing at Philadelphia's Walnut Street Theatre and could hardly have been unaware of this notice which appeared in the *Press:* "We must unquestionably rejoice that popular indignation did not take the shape, which, at one period on Saturday last [April 15, 1865] it seemed likely to do, by inducing the mob which exists in all great cities, even in Philadelphia, to tear down the Walnut Street Theatre, of which Edwin Booth, in conjunction with Clarke, the comic actor, becomes the lessee at the end of the coming summer."

Again, there was the circumstance that she was then under the management of that same Matthew Canning who once had managed John Wilkes Booth. Just a few days before, Booth had seen Canning in an effort to persuade him to join the conspiracy. Perhaps Vestvali knew the assassin as well as his victim. Certainly, in mysterious ways, she was somehow involved in the Lincoln story. But she seems to vanish from it in this line from the Philadelphia *Press,* for April 27, 1865: "Walnut Street Theatre — On account of the illness of Madame Vestvali, 'Uncle Tom's Cabin' was performed at this theatre last evening."

But when she departed from Washington in February, 1864, the fair Felicita could only have left Mr. Lincoln with pleasant memories of her lavish graces. Five days after he had seen her performance, he watched another lady whose history would be part of his. This account was contained in a morning paper for February 9:

Washington Theatre—Eleventh Street. . . . Miss Laura Keene.—The spectacular drama of the "Sea of Ice [or, the Mother's Prayer]" was presented last evening at this establishment to one of the largest audiences ever seen within its walls. The beauty and fashion of our city forming the largest portion of the house. His excellency, the President, with his distinguished lady and family, occupied a private box, and were received with marked applause on their entrance and during the evening. The play was mounted in a manner that elicited the approbation of the entire audience.

Miss Keene's performance of *Ogarita, the Indian Girl,* and her subsequent performance of the lady who resolves to wed the murderer of her mother for the purpose of punishing him, exhibited talent of the highest and most varied order.

The world of the theater was a small world and, by coincidence or destiny, Mr. Lincoln made it smaller still. Late in February Edwin Booth opened an extended engagement at the National, and on Thursday, the twenty-fifth, "President Lincoln and lady" were "highly delighted" by his "powerful rendition" of the title role in John Howard Payne's *Brutus.* The next evening Mr. Lincoln was back again to see Booth as Shylock in *The Merchant of Venice* and as Don Caesar de Byzan. He had received two invitations to that performance, in one of which Mr. Grover had assured him: "Your favorable answer will be taken as a great compliment to the artist"; in the other, Mr. Grover had made the point that the Presidential presence would "place the artiste himself as well as the management under renewed obligations." Directly opposite the President sat the Secretary of State,

Mr. Seward; a critic reported that "the characters . . .
were never better represented than . . . by Mr. Edwin
Booth; this was the universal verdict of the brilliant audience."

Noah Brooks may have mistaken the National for
Ford's, in his "Personal Reminiscences of Lincoln," published in *Scribner's Magazine* for March, 1878, in which
he told of having once gone with the President to see
Edwin Booth in *The Merchant of Venice.*

He was in a remarkable flow of spirits [wrote Brooks], and
made many comical remarks on the progress of the play. . . .
As we sat, two or three of the supernumeraries, who wore
scarlet hose, were constantly in the line of sight. Finally, the
President said, "I wonder if those red-legged, pigeon-toed
chaps don't think they are playing this play. They are dreadful numerous." Just before the act-drop went up each time,
he consulted his programme and said, "This is act two eyes,"
or, "act eye V," as the case might be. And as we went home
he said, "It was a good performance, but I had a thousand
times rather read it at home, if it were not for Booth's playing.
A farce, or a comedy, is best played; a tragedy is best read at
home."

On March 2, it was announced that "by special appointment with the President and Mrs. Lincoln," Booth
would that evening appear in *Hamlet.* Another announcement read:

To-night the special visit of President Lincoln and family
. . . takes place, when the promised performance of "Hamlet" will be given. The double family box usually occupied
by them has been secured for the President and family, and
every preparation has been made by the management to
present the play by an excellent arrangement of the characters

and appointments in a manner every way worthy the extraordinary occasion.

The "command performance" fulfilled the expectations of it. This account appeared on the following morning:

Before twelve o'clock yesterday, every chair in the house had been sold, consequently all who tried to procure seats for the orchestra when the doors opened in the evening were disappointed, and obliged to take themselves to the upper circles, which being filled to a perfect jam before the curtain rose, obliged hundreds to return to their homes without witnessing the play. President Lincoln and family arrived at an early hour, and did not depart until the play was entirely finished, when they like all the brilliant audience, went away delighted almost beyond expression at the rare performance.

On Friday, March 4, the third anniversary of Mr. Lincoln's inauguration, came word:

To-night Mr. Booth will appear, for the last time, in his excellent impersonation of *Richelieu,* in Bulwer's beautiful play of that name, which was to have been presented on Tuesday last, but was postponed to this evening, in accordance with the desires of President and Mrs. Lincoln, who, in consequence of the pre-arranged reception at the Executive Mansion, were unable to attend the theatre on that evening. The President and his worthy lady will be present to-night.

This was prefatory to another sellout. The report read:

This spacious and elegant temple was filled to overflowing, in the true sense of the term . . . Long before the first act . . . was finished, every available foot of space was occupied, and during the evening it is estimated that upwards of one thousand people were turned away from the doors. . . . President Lincoln and family were present during the evening; also Secretary Seward and family.

On Monday, March 7, Mr. Lincoln was again present and in the adjoining box sat Major General Doubleday who, like him, enjoyed a game of ball. The offering was entitled, *The Fool's Revenge,* and Booth "created a new sensation . . . by appearing in a character entirely different from any of his previous representations, and yet one in which his entire force of rare dramatic power is brought to bear in a manner to thrill the souls of every beholder."

But the gala event of Booth's engagement was reserved for Thursday, March 10, when he would appear as Richard III and when the public was informed that—

Lieutenant General Grant has secured a box for this evening, and in honor of this distinguished visitor, Manager Grover has set about preparing every detail for making the occasion the most brilliant by far of the season. President and Mrs. Lincoln and family, and Secretary Seward and family, have also secured boxes and will be present in honor of the event.

On the morrow, however, came this news:

Notwithstanding the heavy storm of last evening, this spacious edifice was crowded far beyond comfort, by one of the most brilliant audiences ever assembled within the walls of a theatre in this city. President Lincoln and family, Secretary Seward and family, Speaker Colfax and several other distinguished heads honored the occasion by their presence. The theatre was tastefully decorated in honor of the distinguished visitors, and with due regard to the promised visit of Lieu-

tenant General Grant with his staff. The names of the different victories of that hero were beautifully inscribed upon different circles and columns of the magnificent auditorium. . . .
That which attracted the most attention was a most magnificent banner, designed and painted by the excellent artist, Mr.
D. A. Strong, in the form of the National colors, beautifully
festooned, over which, surrounded by a wreath of evergreen,
in golden letters, were the words, "Unconditional Surrender."
This, surmounted by a large and splendidly-executed American eagle, and hoisted over the front of the stage, formed one
of the finest and most appropriate designs of the character we
have ever seen. The audience was somewhat disappointed
when Mr. Grover came upon the stage and announced that he
had at a late hour received a note from General Grant, stating
that he could not return from the Army of the Potomac,
where he went in the morning, in time to visit the theatre
that evening; but satisfaction was at once restored when he
announced that a subsequent despatch received from the General assured him that he would be present to witness Mr.
Booth's great impersonation of *Hamlet* this evening. Mrs.
Lincoln has invited the General to occupy a seat in the box
of the President, and his son and staff will occupy the box directly opposite, which was reserved for the General last evening. The President and his household will be present to witness Mr. Booth's representations of the most sublime of all
the immortal Shakespeare's creations, and in which he without a doubt stands without a living equal.

But again the General missed the show; he departed
suddenly for the West, his defection caused by military
exigency. Mr. Lincoln, on the other hand, had given public and visible confirmation to his appreciation of Edwin
Booth's genius, and this regard the actor gratefully returned.

To Mr. Lincoln the importance of the theater was this:
that it provided the only diversion, the only form of recre-

ation he allowed himself in those taut and trying and troublous times. On March 28, 1864, he went to Ford's Theatre to see Edwin Forrest as the Duke of Gloster in *Richard III,* and, when Forrest returned to that stage in the winter of 1865, Mr. Lincoln saw him "three or four times." In February he came twice to Ford's to watch the engaging comedian, John Sleeper Clarke, who had married Asia, sister of Edwin and John Wilkes Booth.

In the light of Mr. Lincoln's subsequent history there is a touch of fatefulness in a petition sent to him by fifty-three players in November, 1864:

A young man, named Oliver B. Wheeler, a member of the Theatrical Profession, is under sentence of death as a deserter from the United States Army.

The Theatrical Profession has furnished a very large number of its members to the Army, and so seldom is an actor guilty of any criminality, that we, the undersigned, Actors and Actresses, beg leave to offer the following extenuating circumstances in the case of Mr. Wheeler.

He was under age when he enlisted, he was ignorant of the grave responsibility he incurred, he is naturally a good natured, unreflecting, foolish boy, who belongs to an excellent family. If you can consistently change his punishment, you will confer a lasting obligation.

Upon receipt of this appeal for executive clemency, Mr. Lincoln telegraphed General Thomas, at Nashville: "Let execution in the case of Oliver B. Wheeler, Sergeant in the 6th Regiment Missouri Vol's., under sentence of death for desertion at Chattanooga, on the 15th inst., be suspended until further order, and forward record for examination."

On the morning of Good Friday, April 14, 1865, came

a messenger from the White House to engage, in the President's name, a box for that evening's performance. It is strange that he elected to see Tom Taylor's play. *Our American Cousin* had been presented several times during the course of his Washington residence and never before had he subjected himself to its banalities. But that night the performance was interrupted. Had Mr. Lincoln, at 10:20, turned his head, he might have recognized the wild figure behind him. The next morning the Lincoln story was finished.

Twenty-four hours later, in Boston, Edwin Booth wrote to his friend, Colonel Adam Badeau, a member of General Grant's staff:

For the first time since the damnable intelligence stunned me that my brother Wilkes enacted this fearful, hellish deed am I able to write and hasten to acquaint you of my existence as it has been so long a time since I last wrote you, making me afraid [of] my silence. You know, Ad, how I have labored since my dear Mary was called from me to establish a name that my child and all my friends wd be proud of; you know how I have always toiled for the comfort & welfare of my family—though in vain, as well you know how loyal I have been from the first moment of this damned rebellion, and you must feel deeply the agony I bear in thus being blasted in all my hopes by a villain . . . who seemed so lovable, and in whom all his family found a source of joy . . . Abraham Lincoln was my President for in pure admiration of his noble career & Christian principles I did what I never did before—I *voted* and FOR HIM!

And on April 22, fifty members of the theatrical profession met in parlor C of Philadelphia's Continental Hotel where they adopted a resolution:

That in the death of Abraham Lincoln we not only mourn as citizens the loss of our revered Chief Magistrate, but also, as professionals, a patron and true friend of our calling and its professors.

They remembered, and perhaps they remembered, too, his fondness for a line from Pope's "Essay": "Act well your part: there all the honour lies."

"In the Presence of the Schollars"

N O T so long ago I came upon a document which arrested my attention. I am still in custody, for that foxed and yellowed leaf is dated November 6, 1848, and relates how learning lighted on a school at Pisgah, situate in Gaston County, state of North Carolina. This is the text, exactly transcribed, of that startlingly revelatory contract:

Articles of agreement in 22 Sde School destrict Between Charles L. Thomison as teacher & Enoch McNair Francis Battie & Alexander Weer Committee in Said Schooll Destrict Ar 1 The Said Charles L. Thomison doath bind Himself to teach by the month at thirteen dollars Per month the afore Said Thomison doath Bind Him Self to teach all the Branches Required By the Schooll acts to be taught in Common Schools

Ar 2 The Said Enoch McNair Francis Battie & Alexander Weer doath bind them Selves to pay to The Said Charles L. Thomison the Sum of thirteen Dollars per month by giving him an Order on the Cheareman of Common Schools

Ar 3 The teacher has the privelege of cloasing the School At the end of any one month or the Committee May Cloase at the end of any month the See proper

Ar 4   School to commence in the morning at the Sun one hour & a half high one hour at intermision and Cloase one hour by Sun Set

Ar 5   All Schollars coming to this School over fifteen Years oald who transgress the rules of Said School Shall Be Expeled by Teacher & Committee

Ar 6   None of the large Schollars Shall Exclude the Smaller Schollars from the benefit of the fire Righting Benches or any other privlege belonging to them in Said School

Ar 7   Thair Shall be no Swareing rastling nor Tale bareing Dureing Said School

Ar 8   Thair is to be no immorall conduct neither By Teacher Nor committee in the presence of The Schollars dureing the above mentioned School

Now, for all I know, committeemen and teachers may be permitted their peccadilloes so long as they are conducted in shuttered privacy, off-duty, and out of hours. But not librarians—we belong to the Glass-House Gang! We are forever "in the presence of the schollars." We must be circumspect—or else.

The inexhaustible Blades told a legend which illustrates our quandary in reverse:

In the year 1439 [wrote William] two Minorite friars, who had all their lives collected books, died. In accordance with popular belief, they were at once conducted before the heavenly tribunal to hear their doom, taking with them two asses laden with books. At Heaven's gate the porter demanded, "Whence came ye?" The Minorites replied, "From a monastery of St. Francis." "Oh!" said the porter, "then St. Francis shall be your judge." So that saint was summoned, and at sight of the friars and their burden demanded who they were, and why they had brought so many books with them. "We are Minorites," they humbly replied, "and we have brought these few books with us as a solatium in the new Jerusalem." "And you, when on earth, practiced the good they teach?" sternly demanded the saint, who read their characters at a glance. Their faltering reply was sufficient, and the blessed saint at once passed judgment as follows: "Insomuch as, seduced by foolish vanity, and against your vows of poverty, you have amassed this multitude of books, and thereby and therefor have neglected the duties and broken the rules of your Order, you are now sentenced to read your books for ever and ever in the fires of Hell." Immediately, a roaring noise filled the air, and a flaming chasm opened, in which friars and asses and books were suddenly engulphed.

For having been diverted from their spiritual exertions, it was no doubt proper that the monks were condemned for all eternity to the Great Books program. But books, ladies and gentlemen, are, temporally at least, a librarian's business. He should respect, honor, revere them. He should know something about them. With some temerity I venture to suggest that he should occasionally even have patience enough to look at them. And if he would serve an earthly penance and thereby assure himself a paradise where there is neither print, nor readers, the librarian should piously bring himself, from time to time, to read a book.

For the librarian is "in the presence of the schollars," and the "schollars" are uneasy. Their suspicions were aroused when first the librarian decided that he had a profession; those suspicions continue to mount; there are moments nowadays when the librarian, oilcan and wrench in hand, interrupts his tinkering and wonders forlornly what has happened to him.

Warnings of popular disfavor came early. In the eighteen eighties, Victoria's subject, Frederick Harrison, expressed a general misgiving in an essay, in which he wrote:

Our human faculties and our mental forces are not enlarged simply by multiplying our materials of knowledge and our facilities for communication. Telephones, microphones, pantoscopes, steam-presses, and ubiquity engines in general may, after all, leave the poor human brain panting and throbbing under the strain of its appliances, no bigger and no stronger than the brains of the men who heard Moses speak, and saw Aristotle and Archimides pondering over a few worn rolls of crabbed manuscript. Until some new Gutenberg or Watt can invent a machine for magnifying the human mind, every fresh apparatus for multiplying its work is a fresh strain on the mind, a new realm for it to order and to rule.

But ah! the apparatus was lovely; it was an end in itself; the caution went unheeded. Then, half a century ago, a New England divine, Gerald Stanley Lee, with his genius for opprobrium, put the so-called "modern" librarian squirmingly on the spot. Wrote Dr. Lee:

They [the modern librarians] are not really down in their hearts true to the books. One can hardly help feeling vaguely, persistently resentful over having them about presiding over the past. One never catches them—at least I never do—forgetting themselves. One never comes on one loving a book. They seem to be servants—most of them—book chambermaids. They do not care anything about a library as a library. They just seem to be going around remembering rules in it.

And Dr. Lee made other unkind accusations, declaring that "So far as I can get at his mind at all, he seems to have decided that his mind (any librarian's mind) is a kind of pneumatic-tube, or carrier system . . . for shoving immortals at people." Dr. Lee went on to say that "Any higher or more thorough use for a mind, such as being a kind of spirit of the books for people, making a kind of spiritual connection with them down underneath, does not seem to have occurred to him." But Dr. Lee conceded that "As a sort of pianola or aeolian attachment for a library, as a mechanical contrivance for making a comparatively ignorant man draw perfectly enormous harmonies out of it (which he does not care anything about), a modern librarian helps."

That was in 1902. In the same year, a youth in the Academic Department of Brooklyn's Polytechnic Institute (his name was William Warner Bishop) indirectly protested so harsh a judgment, writing that "A librarian who is not a lover of books is indeed a sorry specimen of his kind," and insisting that "librarianship does not consist in standard sizes and pneumatic tubes." And the youngster, with that unerring instinct that made him always an elder statesman, posed a rhetorical question: "May we not find in the spirit of the bibliophile one of the bonds which shall hold firmly together the members of our calling now rapidly differentiating to such a degree that we are obliged to flock by ourselves in a yearly increasing number of sections?"

It is interesting but futile to speculate on what might have happened had anyone read Dr. Bishop's essay and had had the hardihood to act upon an excellent suggestion. But, so far as my findings go, it received no attention whatever. Instead . . .

We find in the twenties a distinguished colleague, overwhelmed with the number of books which came under his care, averring "the librarian who reads is lost." His listener, my lamented friend, Francis Huddleston, did not agree. Mr. Huddleston thought it would have been more true had he said, "The librarian who does not read will be found out."

Actually, of course, he was found out long ago; but by some miracle of self-delusion he is either unaware of his exposure or completely immune to its implications.

When, in the pages of *The Library Quarterly,* Randolph Adams, the irreplaceable, added librarians to fire, water, vermin, dust, housemaids, collectors, children and other enemies of books, he credited an eastern member of the guild, with having made, in 1935, the bland pronouncement: "Bookloving is no doubt a noble passion, praiseworthy in business men and other amateurs, but out of place in the temperament of the librarian."

Even so decorous and decorative a spirit as Larry Powell was recently obliged ruefully to admit: "It has been my experience that many of the present generation of library administrators are hardly more than literate."

And Manchester's Louis Stanley Jast, put the finishing touches on the indictment when he told an audience at Birmingham: "We speak of a man of the world, meaning a man who is easily at home in any society in which he finds himself. The librarian must be equally at home in the world of ideas." But, continued Dr. Jast: "The things that so many of them don't know, don't want to know, maybe aren't capable of knowing, are staggering." Dr. Jast supposed "that modern mechanized and unduly stressed vocational education is responsible, together with the revolt against the old-fashioned discipline."

There you have it, ladies and gentlemen. Is the charge well-founded? Have we, thoughtlessly but deliberately, changed a rather lovely, personal art, compounded of imagination, pertinacity, initiative, and the exhilarating joy of the search into a grim and selfless technology? Have we forfeited the fertile fields of bibliography to the barbarians who call themselves documentalists? Have those heathens, Mini and Magni, proselyted us to their strange cult where perversely invisibility is held benign and everything must be reduced before it can regain wholesome dimensions? Have we replaced memory and ingenuity with electric scanners and magic eyes? Are our libraries become no more than intellectual garages? Must we practice our craft only in accordance with strict, inflexible, and anointed procedures? Have centralized cataloging and automatic accession processes removed us to an unlettered world? Have we surrendered our prerogatives to the drugstore clerk behind the counter of paperbacks? If we *have,* ours is a wretched plight indeed.

I do not disregard the plethora of print. I have grown old in acres of arrearage. I am not insensible to the problem of dealing daily with accretions of hundreds and thousands of books. But there is a maxim to the effect that "if you can't lick 'em, jine 'em." This I would paraphrase: if you can't list 'em, read 'em!

Leigh Hunt described our quandary when he wrote: "The idea of an ancient library perplexes our sympathy by its map-like volumes, rolled upon cylinders. Our imagination cannot take kindly to a yard of wit, or to thirty inches of moral observation, rolled up like linen in a draper's shop." He was right. Unless we are resolved to resist the tendency, books in quantity lose their individual identities and become mere commodities, comparable to so many cans of soup on a market counter.

This Hunt was a man who hated "to read in public, and in strange company." Carlyle suffered acutely from what he called "Museum headache." Perhaps our environment discourages us from obedience to our precepts.

But there have been those whom books did not appal. My Lord Bishop of that other Durham, Richard De Bury, old Philobiblon himself, exclaimed, "Oblivions would overcome us had not God provided for mortals the remedies of books." Another man of passion, Casanova, when wearied of more muscular exercise, graciously became librarian at Dux.

It was Charles Lamb, you remember, who inquired why have we not "a grace before Milton—a grace before Shakespeare—a devotional exercise proper to be said before reading the *Fairy Queen?*" And Thackeray, in one of the charming *Roundabout Papers* followed suit when he wrote:

Many Londoners—not all—have seen the British Museum Library. . . . What peace, what love, what truth, what beauty, what happiness for all, what generous kindness for you and me, are here spread out! It seems to me one cannot sit down in that place without a heart full of grateful reverence. I own to have said my grace at the table, and to have thanked heaven for this my English birthright, freely to partake of these bountiful books, and to speak the truth I find there.

Perhaps, after all, there is something to be said for the institutions to which we belong. But how, ladies and gentlemen, how are we to defend, as we are called upon to defend, the freedom of inquiry, the freedom of information, so long as we ourselves do not inquire and are uninformed?

There is nothing for it; we must recapture childhood's habit. We must begin to read again. Reading is very splendid, but when we librarians take it up again, let us be more moderate. The "schollars" are looking and vicariously insist on temperance in all things.

And there was Macaulay, of whom the Reverend Sydney Smith remarked: "There are no limits to his knowledge, on small subjects as well as great; he is like a book in breeches." It seems to me that Macaulay also went too far. It is fine to be crammed with learning and to talk like a page from the *World Almanac,* but among librarians there are far too many women for the world ever to tolerate their being books in breeches. Despite her prevalent disbelief, it is contrary to a law of nature for Madame becomingly to be contained within a pair of pants.

No, if I have persuaded you, if you are determined to recover an ancient, quite forgotten taste, please, I beg you, take it easy. And if you would follow sound counsel, listen to a rising member of Parliament, Arthur James Balfour, delivering the rectorial address at St. Andrews seventy-three years ago:

The best method of guarding against the danger of reading what is useless is to read only what is interesting. . . . He has only half learnt the art of reading who has not added to it the even more refined accomplishment of skipping and skimming; and the first step has hardly been taken in the direction of making literature a pleasure until interest in the subject, and not a desire to spare (so to speak) the author's feelings, or to accomplish an appointed task, is the prevailing motive of the reader. . . . There are times, I confess, when I feel tempted somewhat to vary the prayer of the poet, and to ask whether Heaven has not reserved in pity to this much educating generation some peaceful desert of literature as yet unclaimed . . . where it might be possible for the student to wander, even perhaps to stray, at his own pleasure; without finding every beauty labelled, every difficulty engineered, every nook surveyed, and a professional cicerone standing at every corner to guide each succeeding traveller along the same well-worn round. . . . This world may be kind or unkind, it may seem to us to be hastening on the wings of enlightenment and progress to an imminent millennium, or it may weigh us down with a sense of insoluble difficulty and irremediable wrong; but whatever else it be, so long as we have good health and a good library, it can hardly be dull.

If this be so, how long shall we be dullards? For us, salvation is at hand. We can reach it on our shelves. We can find fellowship with the "schollars" and become again part of a sometimes entrancing company: the noble company of the lettered. And in the words of a manuscript come straight from the Middle Ages:

O Lord, send the virtue of thy Holy Spirit upon these our books; that cleansing them from all earthly things, by thy holy blessing, they may mercifully enlighten our hearts and give us true understanding; and grant that by thy teaching, they may brightly preserve and make full an abundance of good works according to thy will.

Surely we are standing in the need of prayer.

Of More Portentous Sound

IT WAS, I believe, the late Mr. Whittier, who profoundly believed that "what she was is Boston still." Certainly, J. P. Marquand subscribed to that doctrine; he built a literary career around it. But I sometimes wonder. Has there not been *some* alteration, *some* change, *some* new grading up or down? There was, for example, the curious episode, known to history as "The Fenway Incident," which transpired at the Hotel Somerset on Saturday evening, January 12, 1907.

The occasion was the seventh annual convocation of the Boston Authors' Club. For the energetic and gifted entertainment committee, it marked the culmination of weeks of dedicated activity. Invitations had been dispatched to the illustrious membership and to less favored literates at large in other regions, each enclosing two cards on which recipients were asked to indite poetic encomia to the two guests of honor who were, respectively, the Club's President, Mrs. Julia Ward Howe, and her "dear vice," as she called the veep, Colonel Thomas Wentworth Higginson.

These enclosures were a daring innovation. Wrote Dr. Amos R. Wells, editor of the *Christian Endeavor World* and author of *Tuxedo Avenue to Water Street,* who ordered two tickets:

These little cards for our honored leaders are a capital notion. I have filled mine out after a jingling fashion, and here they are.

Harriet Mulford Lothrop, begetter of *The Five Little Peppers,* who wrote in monolithic characters, announced:

I will send you the two little slips for the souvenir today. Heaven only knows what I shall write on them. They seem so innocent and small, but they may lamentably betray us authors, especially those of us who cannot get into an inch of space comfortably! Well—we must do it—and show affection, esteem for the subjects and our own brilliancy in one breath!

Declared Kate Louise Brown, the well-known kindergarten teacher:

I used to write a little poetry when I lived out in the "Rhubarb District." Now that I'm a real urbanite the stream has ceased: I think the electric car gongs are responsible. I'm not very proud of the greetings enclosed though they express at least the fervor of my feeling toward our dear Guests of Honor. I have been driving little pigs all day.

More than sixty persons committed effusive salutations to those tiny cards and what a surpassing anthology they must have made! But, in addition to compiling them, the entertainment committee was stormed with questions. Thus, Mr. Allen French, author of *The Junior Cup,* who dwelt at 200 Commonwealth Avenue, prudently inquired:

Will you kindly inform me how long the dinner—and speeches are expected to last? I have to make plans about getting home.

And some of the respondents were uncertain. From Brookline, Eliza Orne White, whose *A Borrowed Sister* had recently appeared, sent this ambiguous word:

What you said decided me to go to the dinner, and I shall want a ticket, unless Mrs. Aspinwall should give out, which is not probable.

But now days of impatient waiting were over; the festivities could begin. They began promptly at six o'clock in the Somerset's parlors. At the head of the line stood the redoubtable Mrs. Howe who, as Bliss Perry once remarked, had won "fame by one ecstatic lyric." Her portrait, complete with cap, kerchief, pendant cross, beringed fingers, folded hands, a gentle expression on her venerable features, had just been painted for *The Outlook* by Kate Rogers Nowell.

Macaulay's comment to the effect that "some reviewers are of opinion that a lady who dares to publish a book renounces by that act the franchises appertaining to her sex, and can claim no exception from the utmost rigor of critical procedure," certainly did not apply to Mrs. Howe. Hers was a unique position. Tonight she was wearing, inter alia, a corsage of violets and orchids bestowed by another Julia, Julia Marlowe.

At Mrs. Howe's side, sharing the tribute of the faithful, stood that other octogenarian, Colonel Higginson, charming, correct, and courtly as always. Past them filed one hundred and eighteen members and guests. The complete roster has not been discovered but it is known that among them were Thomas Bailey (*Atlantic Monthly*) Aldrich, Professor Edward K. Rand, Harvard's classicist, Samuel T. Pickard, Whittier's literary executor, Charles H. Gibson, whose pseudonym was "Richard Sudbury," Anne Whitney, sculptress, Cyrus E. Dallin, sculptor, William Dana Orcutt, book designer, Nixon Waterman, composer of light verse, William Stanley Braithwaite, lover of newspaper lyrics, Oscar Fay Adams, teacher, Benjamin H. Ticknor, publisher, Kate Gannett Wells, widow, Clyde Fitch, dramatist, William Rideing, of the *Youth's Companion*, Samuel M. Crothers, preacher to Harvard College, and many other notables of comparable eminence.

At seven o'clock the celebrants adjourned to the palm room where, according to the *Herald* version, "tables had been artistically placed about, beneath the myriad of electric lights." There followed a sumptuous repast, featured by a mammoth birthday cake, topped by seven pink candles.

The formal proceedings were initiated by Madame President Howe who delighted the audience with a rhymed address, only recently and especially contrived. I forbear to quote it in extenso, but it sparkled with such stunning lines as:

> So here's to your friendly pledge
> Of volumes gilt to the edge

Of the illustrated book,
Which we read not, but only look,
Of the play that was not played,
Of the hit that was never made. . . .
Yes, 'tis time I stopped;
The hint is already dropped,
And I must hold my tongue
That other songs may be sung.

They were. A spirited quartet rendered "the Battle
Hymn of the Republic" and Colonel Higginson's martial
"Waiting for the Bugle." The Honorable John Davis
Long, former Governor and Secretary of the Navy, eulo-
gized the guests of honor. He, in turn, was followed by
Mrs. Louise Chandler Moulton, who referred to the couple as representing "two of the ideals of my life." Next
on his feet was *The Century's* Richard Watson Gilder.
His presence was particularly gratifying because three
weeks before he had sent his regrets, explaining, "I am
under the weather again—not so that I have to stop work,
but so that I have to stay a good deal at home and keep
away from festivities." Yet there he was, in the flesh, and
speaking feelingly of his appreciation for the lady and the
lady's Colonel.

When Mr. Gilder resumed his seat, Mrs. Howe turned
the silver gavel over to Mr. Nathan Haskell Dole who
presented *The Virginian's* Owen Wister, *Collier's* Nor-
man Hapgood, and the *Transcript's* Edward H. Clement.
But it remained for a Whitman collector, from Rahway,
New Jersey, Miss Carolyn Wells, to express the universal
sentiment. Reading from a manuscript on pale green
stationery, she intoned:

The Boston Authors Club! Oh name profound!
Are there three words of more portentous sound!
Could phrase connote more mental depth or height,
More brilliant brain, more learning, or more light?
More letters, language, literature or lore?
More range of thought, of wisdom greater store?
No! Erudition knows no higher plane
Than B. A. C. can easily attain.

In any event, the party was a great success. Colonel
Higginson regarded it as a "wonderful achievement,"
and years later Maud Howe Elliott would recall how
much her mother had valued that "precious collection of
tributes." Anna Fuller, author of *A Literary Courtship*,
was fulsome in her praise:

As I was leaving the table [she wrote] I met Mrs. Henry
Whitney and remarked that I had never been to a big func-
tion like that before, upon which she replied that she had
never been to so pleasant a one. I think everyone shared that
sentiment.

It had a good press. The *Post* said confidently that "to
all intents and purposes, it was the American Salon of
letters." The *Globe* spoke a little defiantly: "Boston's culture [it proclaimed], the favorite theme of the jokesmiths,
was exemplified in such a way as to leave no room for
jest." The impeccable *Transcript* called it "the most nota-
ble gathering that Boston has seen in many a day."

And yet there had been other notables who had found
it necessary or agreeable to stay away.

A naval historian, Theodore Roosevelt, wrote from the
White House: "I wish I could accept, but it is simply out
of the question"; adding, "I am particularly sorry not to

be present at any celebration held in honor of my dear friend Julia Ward Howe."

Curtis Guild, Governor of Massachusetts, explained: "The very serious illness of Mrs. Guild after her dangerous operation makes it impossible for me even to read your letter to her. I am only going to such *public* functions as I cannot escape just now."

George Ade, the fabulist, was so circumstanced that he could not "unite with your members in doing honor to the two young people who are to sit at the head table."

There were several conflicting commitments: Ruth McEnery Stuart was pledged "to read to an audience in Buffalo." The Winston Churchill who belonged to the Richard Carvel branch of the family, was sorry that "a previous engagement at a small dinner of considerable political importance prevents my accepting the invitation."

E. H. Sothern, the actor, stopping at Boston's Hotel Bellevue, was obliged to decline. "I wish greatly that I might be present on so delightful an occasion [he mourned]—it is my fortune to be greatly occupied at this time on the study of new roles and I am not at liberty to give any time at all to other engagements."

William Vaughn Moody appeared to be a trifle miffed: "I am afraid I can't come," he demurred. "Even if I could surmount the necessity laid upon me of being 'amusing,' and 'for five minutes.' The nonchalance with which you state this staggering condition appalls me, and soothes the sting of my regret with the conviction that even if I could come, I should be rejected. If I could be given a 'thinking part'—! But I must not cherish a craven hope."

Edwin Markham put down the hoe and released his muse: "I greatly regret that the pressure on my time forces me to be absent from your reception in honor of Mrs. Howe and Colonel Higginson—those two young people forever young like Yosemite and the Sphinx. They have ever struck out of life the courageous music of joy. Like the lark grown bold with heaven, may they keep sounding on their valiant message to men."

Helen M. Winslow, author of *Literary Boston Today,* was in angry and reminiscent mood. From Shirley, she let it be known that: "I've been laid up (in bed most of the time) for 3 weeks with the meanest, worst, savagest and altogether ugliest form of the grip and I shall not be able to get to Boston . . . I am particularly sorry as it is the anniversary and—I so well remember going from house to house myself—the December before our formation—getting people like Judge Grant and Colonel H. interested. The latter didn't believe we could make it go, at first, but soon became interested. I worked *very* hard to help start it, and I think it is disappointing that I can't be there to help celebrate."

Henry Blake Fuller, the Chicago cliff-dweller novelist, deplored the fact that "such a trifle as mere distance should prevent my attendance . . . It is on such occasions that we of the West recognize our sad condition as Little Shut-Offs."

The invitation to Florence Earle Coates, president of Philadelphia's Browning Society, and poet-laureate of Pennsylvania by decree of the State Federation of Women's Clubs, was misdirected and arrived too late to allow compliance. Another resident of Philadelphia, Miss

Agnes Repplier, was, as she put it, "hard worked this winter." She could not "spare the time for the journey."

From Amherst, Mabel Loomis Todd, who, with Colonel Higginson, was devoted to the work of Emily Dickinson, replied that "things are too strenuous here this week for anything outside, even this most tempting occasion." Her fellow townsman, Profesor George Bosworth Churchill, was also obliged to stay at home.

Yes, the list of those who forfeited an evening on the Charlesgate Parnassus is long and contains the names of Henry Mills Alden, editor of *Harper's;* the Reverend Edward Anderson, of Quincy; Irving Bacheller, whose *Silas Strong* was moving rather well; John Kendrick Bangs, humorous lecturer and late editor of *Puck;* C. Hanford Henderson, headmaster of the Marienfeld Summer School and author of *The Anatomy of Cheerfulness;* Hannah Kemball, relict; Annie Russell Marble, Thoreau's biographer; Paul Elmer More, Editor of the *Nation;* Kate Douglass Riggs, of Sunnybrook Farm; Franklin Benjamin Sanborn, biographer of Mrs. Howe's late husband; Francis Hopkinson Smith, artist and author; Princeton's Professor Henry van Dyke; and George Edward Woodbury, the learned editor of Poe.

These had been chosen, these had been called; yet, for one reason or another, they had elected not to heed. Their absence was confounding, inexplicable, almost absurd; no satisfactory solution could be discovered. It was hardly likely that these mass abstainers had been reading *that* book.

But exactly two months and twelve days before the soirée at the Somerset, a New York publisher had, through some lapse of taste, issued *The Future in America: A Search After Realities,* by Mr. H. G. Wells. It had contained this slanderous passage:

There broods over the real Boston an immense effect of finality. One feels in Boston, as one feels in no other part of the States, that the intellectual movement has ceased. Boston is now producing no literature except a little criticism. Contemporary Boston art is imitative art, its writers are correct and imitative writers, the central figure of its literary world is that charming old lady of eighty-eight, Mrs. Julia Ward Howe. One meets her and Colonel Higginson in the midst of an authors' society that is not so much composed of minor stars as a chorus of indistinguishable culture.

No, Mr. Wells's outrageous strictures could hardly account for the defection. Authors, then as now, did not read books in print. There must have been another, a more persuasive explanation. But there were some among the stay-aways who bravely, brazenly bore their misfortunes. A charter member, who shall be nameless here, was one of those reconciled to forfeiting the feast. He had to be in Washington on that incandescent Saturday. In a whispered acknowledgment, he wrote:

Entre nous, I am not sorry that I have such an impregnable excuse for not being present. . . . In case I send you a telegram expressing my disappointment . . . you may show the crocodile tears between the lines to Owen Wister but to no one else. I dare not tell you on paper all which I feel about the Authors' Club of Boston. It reminds me among other things of the snakes in Ireland. But I am no Mr. Wells. . . .

I venture to write this flippantly (or rather truthfully) because, while you did not write in a spirit of gloom exactly, I detected no traces of rampant enthusiasm in your announcement that the Boston Authors' Club is to have another dinner. You can't very well read this at the dinner because it would expose me to proceedings by Mr. Moran or some other protector of Authors' Clubs, but if I can find time, I will send you something to explain my absence and preserve the conventions of society. But this is my heart-felt paean of joy at my fortunate escape.

With shameless duplicity, the heretic *did* send something; this was it:

> If man could change the universe
> By force of epigrams in verse,
> He'd smash some idols, I allow,
> But who would alter Mrs. Howe?

But we must ask ourselves, were the scoffer's chidings of the Boston Authors' Club as flippantly truthful as he protested? Did he really mean to disparage Boston's literary grandeur? Or did he subsequently and suddenly repent? Or was his, like those of the other absentees, a flashing, quickly fading, aberration? How could he know then that a few years hence he in propria persona would preside over the office now held by Mrs. Howe, or that when he would reach threescore years and ten, the Club would honor him as now it was honoring her, with Mr. Orcutt as toastmaster for *his* symposium and speeches by Robert Bridges, Bliss Perry, Basil King, Alice Brown, and William Roscoe Thayer? Whatever the explanation may be, it is clear that for that tragic moment he felt aloof, and reckoned not with Boston's subtly puissant charm. Boston has a way of bringing cynics to themselves.

I close the recital on a note of supplication. I have searched the record and have been horrified to find the name of only a single librarian, a resident of Providence, who was summoned to the Somerset. Professional pride forbids me to divulge his identity, for that graceless miscreant not only had the temerity to decline, but was so discourteous, so insensitive, so unimaginative, so forthright, so strictly honest as to present not even the flimsiest excuse. This is degrading, and I lay bare the truth with a prayer that you will charge me with no fault more heinous than attempted atonement, retribution, and belated amends.

The Community of Greatness

IT MIGHT be just as well if suddenly and fixedly there came to our governors, our enemies, and other comptrollers of destiny the realization that his most excellent majesty, the American, is irrepressibly, intuitively, and irresistibly a romantic intruder. In the glorious company of his saints, the gate-crasher and the arbiter of manners occupy important places; one helps him gain admittance to the inner circle, the other endows him with grace to make him welcome when, at last, he bursts into the charmed society. Strangely overlooked by the historians is the fact that the abolition of slavery was simultaneously attended by the abolition of the barbaric doctrine of equality. In the land of the free, mediocrity was forever outlawed, and the race became, however paradoxically, a race of snobs liberated from the degradation of toadyism. An American poet wrote "Excelsior" and an American politician wrote "Every Man a King." Not imitation, therefore, but emulation became the first article of faith. This is a surpassing country now, where the private lives of public figures have been completely nationalized, and nationalization has produced the community of greatness. Traces of it are easily discernible in literature.

The Old World may keep its Romeo and Juliet, its Pelleas and Melisande, its Troilus and Cressida, its Hero and Leander, its Antony and Cleopatra; young America has for lovers its Panegyric and Panacea and likes them very much. No hopeless passion theirs, but what it lacks in tender sadness is more than compensated by robust popularity. These characters are sometimes given modern names and strut about in modern versions but their story is always the same story in whatever form it is repeated. It is repeated now.

For the student of the quiet past, poring over elaborate vance-packardiagrams, comes soon the knowledge that *mores* are unchanging, that promotion is and long has been the gentle art of name-dropping, and that it is important to associate products with personages drawn from entrants in Debrett's *Peerage,* the *Social Register,* or Anthony Hollywood's *Athenae.* Thus, not very long ago, it was possible to find in the public prints enthusiastic tributes to miraculous cosmetics paid by such impeccable and exclusive ladies as Mrs. George Jay Gould, Nina Spencer (then a New York debutante) Locke, and Mrs. David Anthony Drexel. Elizabeth Taylor, at least before her marriage to Mr. Fisher, found Clear Red No. 3 just the thing for her brunette coloring. Jane Russell was betraying her beauty secret: Jergen's. Donna Reed urged her sex to "Be Lux lovely all over." Ann Sheridan was slimming "the way the stars slim"—with Ayds. Mrs. Robert P. Gibb, hostess and horse-woman of Far Hills, New Jersey, found Herbert Tareytons completely compatible with her discriminating taste.

To-day Shelley Winters and Jimmy Stewart publicly proclaim the virtues of Air France; a New York photographer asks the purely rhetorical question, "Who 'shot' the President of the Ritz-Carlton Hotel Company?"; ambassadors and Academy Award winners ride the Super Chief; la Brigitte Bardot gets "pure allure" in her eyes with the help of Aziza; Le Marquis and La Marquise de Pins enjoy the hot hors d'oeuvres served on the United States Lines; the Princess Wilhermina Borghese, models a dark (ripe?) olive dress, with bias-cut bodice, which may be acquired in facsimile from Lord and Taylor, New York, or Julius Garfinckel, Washington; Mrs. Rosemary Murphy ("Mrs. America"), of Kentland, Indiana, is pictured in her Naturalizer wardrobe; Enid Boulting, "one of the most exciting women in the world," excitedly insists that "Pond's keeps my skin clear and smooth"; Mike Nichols and Elaine May are background for Smirnoff Vodka; Clare Boothe Luce prettily defends the Great Books and their Syntopicon. In honor of the great awakening aroused by the Civil War Centennial, National Distillers have invoked the shades of a Confederate, John Hunt Morgan, and a Unionist, Ulysses S. Grant, I, in valiant defense of Old Crow. Now, as always, the charms of soaporifics are proundly pronounced by the illustrious and the clear-complexioned. Madison Avenue has entrée to our best people.

No wonder that Panacea, herself a signer of the Declaration of Skin Dependence, and surrounded by such elves, should, whatever her guise and manifestation, exercise without restraint her mythological powers. For the cult of beauty is the essence of American culture and is stimulated by the personal touch. Yet, strangely, the foreign office has overlooked its blandishments in the conduct of international cultural relations. Just suppose that the "Voice" let it be known that Mr. K. uses Mennen's lotion, would not his authority, then and there, vanish quite away? Again, if some forlorn little baggage in the Urals were to have pressed into her grubby hand a tube of Clear Red No. 3, with warranty of being at once a *femme fatale,* would not bomb production suddenly diminish? Or, again, if some female Ubangi could render herself less offensive to the warrior of her choice, would not peace come firmly to the jungle? Of course it would and, of course, if Pond's cold cream had been generally available on the counters of Sparta, Menelaus would not have been constrained dubiously to defend his dubious honor. Mrs. Drexel's formula would have reconciled him. There would have been too many Helens thereabout.

Now here in the United States, here in the community of greatness, there is nothing particularly new in lyrical addresses to merchandise and the pervasion of rouge. Neither is there anything particularly new in the association of reputations and commodities. Ladies and gentlemen of distinction have, for a long time, publicly presented their images and encomia in behalf of products which reflect in one way or another the simple elegance of their taste. To be invited to write a testimonial for an alluring product is *really* to have arrived! I do not, it is true, recall any celebrity who has let it be known that she uses this or that salve for the relief of persistent acne, or one who proclaims the virtues of a drug for soothing athlete's foot, but where the object is itself desirable there is always a ready witness to endorse it. The satisfied customer, identified as favorable, attractive, and in the flesh, is part of the American way of life.

Out of that way has grown the art which counted, among its early practitioners, my unfortunate old friend, Professor Gardner. My knowledge of him is admittedly imperfect; many biographical details have so far eluded me; but he is nevertheless possessed of such fascination that I would be selfish not to share my enchantment.

The Professor emerged for me from the second page of the *Cleveland Daily Herald* for March 9, 1851:

D. P. Gardner [read an announcement] known as the New England Soap Man, purposes to Lecture in Cleveland on his favorite topic, some evening this week. He is a Yankee genius of the oddest genus, and soaps everybody but editors. They belong to the class bored.

N. B. The Soap Man goes off at Empire Hall to-morrow evening.

Hear the *Detroit Tribune* descant on his manner and mission:

We heard [wrote the Detroit reporter] D. P. Gardner, the New England "Soap Man" last night. By Jove, he's great— Talk of Cicero and Demosthenes—but then, they hadn't such a subject.

Not all the soap he will sell during his mortal career, will wash out the remembrances of having seen and heard him. We are not puffing the soap man; we cannot puff him. Moreover he's past and gone, as far as that's concerned, (to be sure, we may as well tell you that he remains till Monday, to bestow favors on mankind, at a shilling a face, clean one.) But we regard him philosophically. Such men as this, form one of the grand "items" of civilization. We shall give our views on it in a day or two. In the mean time we have to return him our sincere thanks for having made us laugh—joyously and happily—and is not that something to be grateful for? Answer me, you whose spirits are broken, and hearts oppressed with the gnawing cares of worldly striving.

Man is only happy inasmuch as he blesses others; then, will each vernal "grease" spot be erased from the soap man's soul —peace to his "ashes."

The next day Clevelanders were greeted with the news:

Gardner "goes and does it" tonight, at Empire Hall, and those who like a good lecture and desire to be posted up as to the history and good qualities of soap will be there to listen. Admittance gratis. Children under ten years of age, half price. Front seats reserved for Editors.

Perhaps it should be interjected here that the salubrious saponification, hawked by this latter-day Savonarola at twelve and a half cents a cake, contained astonishing properties:

Prof. Gardner's Soap [read a prospectus] will make a splendid Lather; it removes Paint and Grease from Garments, and Pimples from the Face; cures the worst Chapped Hands in two days. It is better for the Teeth and Gums than any tooth powder you can find, and the taste is pleasant.

The lecture went off well; the audience roared; it was noted that "he has in him the elements of fun and he lets those elements loose." But despite his geniality, there was a Barnum-Bunyanesque quality in him. Like Barnum he was not above a spoof; like Bunyan his zeal was frequently mistaken for something less commendable, and, still like Bunyan, he was a "vagrant oft in quod." There

were, I am very much afraid, some embarrassing episodes
in his career from which a less resourceful master could
not so deftly have extricated himself. One occurred the
following weekend and was chronicled in these terms:

Gardner was in Akron on Saturday, and had just selected a
favorable location for holding forth . . . when a newly
elected constable tapped him on the shoulder and enquired if
he was aware of the penalty for selling without a license.
Gardner allowed that he would hold a private audience with
the Mayor before he made sale of any of his cakes, and accordingly straddled for the office.

The Mayor pointed out the law—a fine of not more than
one hundred dollars for selling, crying or disposing of goods,
wares and merchandise, at vendue without a license. "But,"
said Gardner, striking an attitude, "does your honor for a
moment suppose that I, Soap Gardner, a lineal descendant, in
an air line, of that glorious Puritan, Awful Gardner, who
landed on the everlasting hills of New England from a discon-
solate fishing smack, that I am in the eagle eye of the law, crying goods, wares or merchandise, when I am impressing upon
the minds of the denizens of Ohio's Summit, that nothing else
would so greatly conduce to their welfare and happiness in
the present, or to their peace of mind and success in the future, as the purchase of my soap . . . ? Does your honor for
a moment suppose, that standing on the dividing line which
separates ages that are past from those which are to come, and
the solemn thought that an hundred years hence, sliding down
the well soaped ways of Time . . ."

"Hold on you descendant of Awful Gardner," shouted the
Mayor, "you *can't* violate any statute of Ohio, sell when and
where you please, and if any officer interferes, soap his eyes
and proceed."

It is interesting to speculate on the Professor's allusion
to an ancestor. Certainly the introduction of Awful Gard-

ner was intended only to confuse, for "Awful" Gardner, whose parents long ago had inflicted on him the name of Orville, was a notorious contemporary and, as an evangel, a competitor of the Professor's. A prize fighter and reformed drunkard, "Awful" was at that very moment engaged in bringing thousands of derelicts to redemption along New York's New Bowery. But early in the seventeenth century, in 1624 to be exact, the Dorchester Company in England sent colonists to establish a plantation of fishermen at Cape Ann which included a Thomas Gardner. Because of poor soil, the plantation was not a success; many of the adventurers returned to Britain, while Thomas and a few of his hardier fellows moved on to form a new settlement called Salem and to become forebears of a hardy breed. Eventually, in 1823, Richard Gardner, great-great-great-great-grandson of Thomas, and his wife Eliza, were blessed with an heir whom they called Daniel Pierce Gardner. The author of the family history was never able to learn what became of Danny. Perhaps he grew up to be the peddling Professor who was not one to stay put or to leave a trace.

As to his academic status there is some confusion. While once a visitor in Springfield, it was solemnly announced in the *Illinois State Journal* (no doubt with his acquiescence and approval) that he was a professor at Brown University. But, strangely enough, the archives of the university contain no confirmation of the claim. Perhaps his faculty affiliation was with Clown.

It is of record, however, that he departed the Middle West on Wednesday evening, July 16, 1851, when he boarded the Empire State bound for Buffalo. On that vessel, it was said at the time, that he would "run her, for this trip only, entirely by soap power, with lye in the boilers," and that he would "lather any boat that gets in his way." Thereafter, for several years his precise itinerary is uncertain, but in November, 1859, he was back in Cleveland, and carrying on as usual. There was another lull and then the *Indianapolis Daily Sentinel* for August 2, 1860, flashed a tantalizingly meager account:

Professor Gardner [it declared] the New England Soap Man . . . has, by invitation, addressed several Legislative bodies— our own among the number (complimentary votes having been passed in his favor),—has been received with distinguished consideration by the notabilities of the world,— . . . has addressed the largest audiences in every civilized country, who have listened with pleasure to his oratory; and last, but not least, . . . has called forth the encomiums of the Louisville Journal, and all the leading newspapers in the land, for his learning, eloquence, and gentlemanly accomplishments.

Professor Gardner has twice visited Europe, and gained the medals at the World's Industrial Exhibitions at London and Paris, and he has in his possession certificates from the ablest scientific men in the world as to the purity and excellence of his Soap.

The lectures of Professor Gardner are of an elevated and intellectual character; and although they abound in wit and humor, it is of that chaste and faultless style that the most delicate and refined lady may listen to them without dread of having the blush called to her cheek. Indeed, as a lecturer he is extremely popular with the ladies, who delight in his poetical and humorous images.

The Professor himself could hardly have done better than that, perhaps he did *do* it, and neglected only to mention the extensive correspondence in which he was constantly engaged. But what gave the *Sentinel* article

particular importance was the Professor's "correct like-
ness" which embellished it. The subject sat for that portrait, and wore for the occasion a double-breasted coat
with velvet collar, a flowing tie, a gold watch chain with
cross dependent spread across a well-pressed vest, and a
ring upon the fourth finger of his left hand which rested
daintily on trousers that may well have been made of
tweed. In his right hand he held, in the posture later
made famous by Doctor Munion, an object which resem-
bled a hearing aid, but which must, in reality, have been
a bar of his magic foil for dirt. The face above the costume was earnest, a firm chin, compressed lips, nose long
and thin as became a Puritan, piercing eyes, a heavy
brow, slightly protruding ears—and topping the black
hair was an altogether startling and mysterious cover.
A Hoosier hatter, to whom I have turned for explanation
of that dome-shaped covering, has expressed the opinion
that it "looks like nothing so much as the headpiece used
in connection with the electric chair." But another school
of experts, composed of Baker Street Irregulars, regard it
as an early model of the cap made fashionable by Dr.
Watson's Mr. Holmes. Quite clearly, however, the flaps
knotted neatly above the visor could be used to protect the
auditory organs from frostbite, or, if fastened beneath the
chin, to hold it securely in place no matter what manner
of eggs were hurled against it.

In any event, Indianapolis wildly feted the admirable
Professor, but alas, e'er long the wanderlust drove him
forth from that gorgeous glade and carried him back to
scenes of earlier triumph. Perhaps professional rivalry
made relaxation impossible. Enoch Morgan's Sapolio and
Colgate's "German Mottled" were turning up in the ad-

vertising columns of the public prints. Their complacent claims could only have agitated the Professor's crusading spirit and called forth new, unparalleled exertions for the cause.

On Friday evening, November 30, at the city of Detroit, the Saint Andrew's Society foregathered for its annual meeting in the Michigan Exchange. The attendance was numerous and "an extraordinary amount of good feeling prevailed among the members." Supper was served at nine o'clock, the tables spread "with the profusion of viands usual to such occasions" and decorated with "two vases of elegant wax flowers" contributed by a generous lady. "After the appetite was satisfied, fruits and wines were introduced." Toasts were drunk to the day, to the Queen of Great Britain, the President of the United States, the Governor of the state of Michigan, the Mayor and Common Council of the city, "our sister societies," and many others likewise laudable and friendly, were potably propitiated. But the felicities were marred by a sobering and untoward incident.

While the speeches and flow of sentiment were at their height [so runs a grim account] a person who has afflicted the city, and more especially the newspapers, with his presence during the past few weeks—a self-styled "Professor Gardner" —took occasion to intrude with a desire for speech. His pretensions imposed upon a gentleman (we are charitable enough to suppose so) who introduced his name to the company, and was met by a decided repulse. A few hisses brought Mr. James Black [a local merchant] to his feet, and in brief and concise terms, Professor Gardner received his quietus. He was informed that, if he wanted to advertise his soap, he would do better to seek a more appropriate locality. It is needless to say

that the quondam "Professor" was squelched, and that he retired in precipitation.

Armed with an unparalleled stock of impudence, a couple
of bogus medals, and a paste breastpin of huge dimensions,
this individual has imposed himself on the community for ten
years, and, by the aid of an over-indulgent press, has acquired
a tolerated position, which is brought into play on every occasion to aid in the attainment of respectable society. Stale joke
and unlimited brass are the qualifications which have elevated
the man and his worthless wares, and an equal stock of vanity
leads to the presumption that sensible people [do not] recognize the fact. Sensible newspapers and sensible people will
put such assumption where it belongs, as the Saint Andrew's
Society did on Friday night.

Clevelanders shared Detroit's indignation. It was said,
then, that he was "played out" and would not dare publicly to show himself again. He had been turned out not
so long ago from the Angier House for his "unwarrantable intrusion" upon the lady guests. As one who never
"called the blush to the cheek," the Professor's sensitive,
chivalrous soul must have been wounded by such treatment. Discouraged but not dismayed, he probably turned
eastward, for two years later came word that—

Professor Gardner . . . whose history . . . has been one
of constant vicissitude . . . has turned up in the vicinity of
"the hub of the Universe," and is to give one of his "thrilling
lectures" at Tremont Temple.

Did he rehabilitate himself and his reputation in the
land of his forefathers? There is every reason to suppose
that somehow, indomitably, devoutly, cheerfully he did,
for he had crashed the community of greatness. The last I

ever heard of him was in a *Message to the People of the United States and Elsewhere,* a document part ukase and part will and testament which he released in 1870. Reading that superb recital of faith and conviction it is impossible to avoid a sense of shame for the generation which so cruelly misjudged, misunderstood, and maligned him. It is filled with lofty sentiment and expressions of such impeccable nobility as to command honor and respect and restoration to a niche of grandeur. These are extracts:

I never drink any spirituous or malt liquors, wine, beer, or cider. I never use profane or vulgar language. I never smoke, take snuff, chew tobacco, nor vote the *Democratic* ticket.

I believe in progress. The wise man's eyes are in his head so that he may look forward and not backward. . . . I believe in our country; all of it as it is, as it is to be, and as it ought to be, bounded north by Freedom, east by Education, south by Equality, west by Progress, washed by four oceans, and *blessed with Gardner's soap.*

I believe in the Bible to be the word of God. . . . I believe the Boston Daily Journal to be one of the most *reliable, high-toned,* and largely circulated secular newspapers in New England, and that whoever reads a copy of it every day, together with a chapter in the Bible; with careful attention, will be sure to vote the straight Republican ticket, even if prohibition against rum-selling and rum-drinking is attached to it. . . .

I believe in myself. The man who does not believe in himself is a fool or a knave. I am neither. I believe that my soap is the best for the price, and the cheapest for the quality, now existing on the face of the globe. And calling upon my friends to support me, and thereby benefit themselves, I pledge to the principles herein set forth, their lives, their fortunes, and their sacred honor.

Now if anyone would possess himself of that sublime creed it would be necessary to obtain a copy of a little brochure of thirty-odd pages entitled *Genuine Autograph Letters From the Most Distinguished Men of Our Country Presented to Professor Gardner*. Produced by the Railway Steam Printing Works, on Boston's Washington Street, it was originally intended as a gift to every purchaser of four cakes of the "unrivalled soap." The sensitive reader has only to examine that fragile pamphlet poignantly to understand the Professor's tragedy. For he was born too soon, and out of prematurity came wretchedness threefold.

In the first place, of course, was the condign circumstance that he lived so long ago as to miss the pretty signatures of Mrs. Gould and Mrs. Drexel and Miss Spencer (as was). Indeed there is nowhere in it a feminine flourish, no eyes of azure stare out of it, no ivory-white hand passes cigarettes, no cheek of riotous coloring is turned. Instead of giddy glamour, only homely *homines* are there. The party is strictly stag and quite unbeautiful. Many of them are Governors of the so-called Loyal States: Burnside, of Rhode Island, sure that, as he wrote, "you will continue to prosper as long as you present so valuable an article to the public"; Andrew, of Massachusetts, a little stiff and formal; his successor, Bullock, less moderate, even fulsome, "I desire to say that in its use I have discovered the elementary, practicable, and appreciable qualities which have elicited the commendation of so many, and intelligent persons"; Buckingham, of Connecticut, "I find it . . . excellent"; Willard, late of Indiana, "I am free to introduce you, after ten years' acquaintance, to all my friends, as a gentleman"; Chamberlain, of Maine, "I trust it may lead some to the rewards of Him that hath clean hands and a pure heart"; Harriman, of New Hampshire, "I can cheerfully recommend it . . . as fully equal to the representations made"; Curtin, of Pennsylvania, "My family pronounce it, in all respects, superior"; Dennison, of Ohio, "I take pleasure in adding my testimony to its valuable properties"; and several others.

The glassmaker, Erastus Corning, is there, and Chester Chapin, president of the Boston and Albany Railroad. There are seconding sermons from the pulpits: the Reverend Enoch Pound, president of the Theological Institute of Bangor, "May you be greatly prospered in your endeavors"; Dr. Thomas Starr King, of the Hollis Street Church in Boston, "If, as some one has said, cleanliness is next to godliness, the Professor is doing a good moral work in the community"; and a letter from Brooklyn, reading:

I have appointed my wife and children a jury to try the merits of your *Soap*. I can have no doubt what their verdict will be. I hope that you will be successful in your mission. Indeed, cleanliness is a moral virtue, and you must be regarded as a missionary of cleanliness to all poor wretches left in the heathenism of dirt.

But if he really believed that, why did Henry Ward Beecher pass the buck to the "Missus and the kids"?

Henry W. Bellows comments: "If you manufacture your *hard* as economically as you do your *soft,* you cannot fail to realize a large fortune in a short time—I wish your *other* factory was as locomotive as the one that walked into my room last evening." Cash Clay sputters: "May the unterrified be persuaded, and the great unwashed become the reverse! Never say die!" Carl Schurz, bound for Spain and breathing heavily above his quill, finds a crowded moment for autobiography with this: "During a fall campaign, the like of which never was seen in this country, it kept my hands clean of dirty bargains, and my face free from long hair; and I indulge in the expectation that over on the other side of the ocean, where I shall procure it at whatever cost it may be, I shall have an opportunity to show the European barbarians what a Yankee can do in the way of Soap." In similar vein, a prominent journalist takes pen in hand:

Years ago, when I was young and green, I made some resolute, even if ill-directed efforts, to reform and renovate the world. They failed, probably for want of preliminary and simultaneous application of soap. You, I perceive, are strong just where I was weak . . . you are younger than I, and have probably discovered the cause of my failure, and have resolved to succeed by avoiding or correcting my error. Go ahead, then Professor! Renovate mankind if you can; but if you can not, at least cleanse and purify them. For your success in that wholesome, if not profoundly searching operation you have the best wishes of

Yours,
Horace Greeley

Among others in attendance are Admiral Farragut, General Howard, John B. Gough, and Petroleum V. Nasby. A Negro, Frederick Douglass, is among the witnesses:

Yes, with all my heart I can commend your excellent Soap. Its effect upon the skin is admirable. While I cannot say that it will wash a black man white, I will say it comes as near to it as any article I ever used. I commend it to all men, and to men of all colors, whether black or white, or those who incline to the copper color.

Congressman Deming indites a letter to a fade-proof General:

Permit me to introduce to you, and commend to your favorable regard, Professor Gardner, a distinguished man himself, and honored with the acquaintance of all men of distinction. The field upon which he has won his honor is his campaign against *dirt,* and the instrument of conquest which he uses is a famous Soap, the merits of which he will detail to you, both in prose and verse. You will find the Professor an accomplished humorist, whom not to know argues yourself unknown.

The General's letter, written two days later, is reproduced in facsimile:

I acknowledge [it begins] the receipt of four cakes of your highly recommended soap which you have been kind enough to leave at my office.

The many testimonials you have of its merits are a sufficient guarantee of its good quality.

> Yours truly
> /s/ U. S. Grant
> General

Another message in facsimile brings encouragement from a candidate. It is written at Springfield, September 28, 1860, and this is the burden of it:

Some specimens of your Soap have been used at our house and Mrs. L. declares it is a superb article—She at the same time protests that *I* have never given sufficient attention to the "soap question ["] to be a competent judge.

Yours truly

A. Lincoln

Well, there you have it! Nothing but ugly old men! But what old men! And how steadfast the theme!

So much for the first aspect of the Professor's tragedy; the second may be more briefly stated: he permitted his business to interfere with the joys and emoluments of autograph collecting. This was a forfeit of virtuosity.

The third aspect is, perhaps, more pitiable than the others. It is more pitiable because it is concentered upon the Professor's horrible, horrifying, horrendous loneliness. As a consequence his residence in the community of greatness was always brief. Isolated, unappreciated, a victim of brittle friendships, untutored in the art, misguided in his searching, sacrificed to impatience and pettiness and petulance, he was, as he said, neither knave nor fool, but he was terribly, pitiably alone.

This being so, suppose that on his last Saturday there came a knock upon his tenement door and suppose on opening it he found a lady standing there in the pale light of the alley. He would, I think, apologize for his shabby attire, and her eyes would glisten in amusement at his shining medals and strange breastpin. She would inquire of him his name and, being satisfied, would hand him a folded sheet of yellow paper which her late husband, a General Parker (a full-blooded Indian), had bade her to deliver when his own use for it had passed. And suppose as he started up the stairs, there came another knock, and, returning, he found there another lady, another widow as unkempt as he and calling herself Bixby. And suppose this other explained her wretchedness: she must have soap, she had no money, she had only this which she would barter. And suppose that this was a piece of whitish paper and that her wish for his celebrated, his cherished product made him then unconscious of the thin exchange. He would, I think, have given her the soap, and shakily would have climbed the stairway to his attic room which Charles *double-d* Addams might have drawn. And suppose that there he would have unfolded the yellow paper and found on it in penciled characters the terms of Capitulation which a Union commander had handed an adversary once at Appomattox. And suppose the writing on the other leaf began "Dear Madam, I have been shown in the files of the War Department . . ." Yes, it would be nice to think that the Professor became at last a real collector before he died.

The Infatuate Wish

WHETHER this be atonement for sin or attainment of grace, I cannot tell. Strangely, carelessly, shamelessly I am called on to expatiate upon a controversial subject with which I have grown increasingly unfamiliar and remote as the years have gathered. Perhaps, in consequence, I should begin with the prayer with which Giovanni Boccaccio, a gentleman not best remembered for his piety, concluded the Preface to his *Genealogia Deorum Gentilium,* and ask that I, too, "may follow a course redounding to the splendor, laud, honor, and eternal glory of His name; but to all detractors confusion, ignominy, disgrace, and eternal damnation!"

In his case, as in mine, it had been a reluctantly accepted assignment. He had complained of the "infatuate wish of the Ancients to be considered descendants of gods." He had protested that "this foolish faith . . . flourished everywhere." He had conceded the fact that "here a book and there another has something to say on the subject," but, he asked, "who is there that would wish, for no useful result, or at least for very little, to hunt them all up, read, and finally gather a few notes?"

Come, Giovianni, how utterly mistaken can you be! Actually, there are thousands of these odd seekers. Overseas, in the New-found Worlde, the cult hath banded together in a national society and annually doth make wassail, leaning heavily on the bar—that is to say, leaning heavily on the bar dexter,—feasting on relationships *au jus*, and harking to a dullard's drones.

As to the literature of lineage, Giovanni, it has grown at a reckless, rapid pace in the brief period of a half-millennium. Books wear out under the frenzied eyes of night prowlers, more intent on knowing whence they came than whither they are going. Pages grow brittle and break away from much turning. Ink blurs from the constant rubbing of countless thumbs. Bindings crack and covers fall away. But the taste for tracings, however eccentric it may be, is popular and insatiable. Neither the sobering preachments of Dr. Darwin nor the disquieting formulae of Father Mendel have managed to allay it.

Libraries, Giovanni, pander to this extraordinary craze. Such an one is perched upon the Capitoline Hill in the new City of Washington. One hundred and forty-five years ago, it purchased the collection of a political character, one Thomas Jefferson, who enjoyed some prominence at the time. There were, I am happy to say, a few brave spirits who resisted that unseemly acquisition. It would, they feared, contain books which might be described as of an "atheistical, irreligious, and immoral tendency." Their objections might have been sustained had they but known that it included a good edition of *Domesday Book*,

Le Neve's *Monumenta Anglicana,* Kimber's *Peerage,* and other genealogical sources.

That was the beginning. Then in the eighteen seventies a foolish librarian who called himself Ainsworth Spofford, secured from an equally foolish Congress a special appropriation of five thousand dollars for the purchase of English County histories and in no time at all this graceless man Spofford reported that "all but seven, out of the forty counties of England, are now represented in the Library, besides many of the town histories, and the local histories and genealogies of Ireland, Scotland and Wales." Without a touch of uneasiness or guilt, he went so far as to justify his action by explaining that "the great interest of these works, and their value as elucidating the history and genealogy of that country from which most American families derive their origin, together with the fact that the most extensive county histories were printed in small numbers and are constantly rising in price, render this a wise and timely purchase." Still unblushingly, he announced: "It is satisfactory to add that the cost of the collection (including what were already in the Library) will come well within the limits of the appropriation."

When, a few years later, I joined the Library's staff and was consigned to parading around the central desk in that marbled octagon which is the Reading Room, the situation had got entirely out of hand. For years these ancient arms of mine were daily wearied and withered from lifting, without respite or relief, Durrie and its supplement, Marshall, Burke, Rietstaps, the immortal work of Bishop Meade and other ponderous, clue-giving compendia.

In my youth, Giovanni, I was not aware of the mischie-

vous caprices which characterize the classifiers of knowledge. Being innocent, I reasoned then that genealogy
might be considered a branch of biology, or of anthro-
pology, or of animal husbandry where the stud books
were, or of the social sciences to which sex was cheerfully
assigned, or of religion and philosophy which were said
to comprehend mythology. Imagine if you can my everlasting consternation when I discovered that genealogy
was allocated a place among the auxiliary sciences of history.

As I have said, it *is* a controversial subject. The Apostle
Paul, in his first letter, admonished Timothy: "Neither
give heed to fables and endless genealogies, which minister questions, rather than godly edifying which is in
faith." In writing to Titus he warned him to "avoid foolish questions, and genealogies, and contentions, and striv-
ings about the law; for they are unprofitable and vain."

Strangely enough the Saint from Tarsus, who has been
given Scriptural authority, is supported from another perspective by Ambrose Bierce in *The Devil's Dictionary*
where genealogy is said to be a noun and is defined as
"an account of one's descent from an ancestor who did
not particularly care to trace his own."

And there have been outrageous scoffers. Horace Wal-
pole, in a letter to the Countess of Upper Ossory, dated
August 27, 1783, betrayed the shocking levity of his mind
by writing:

I should be mortified to have had any genuine Fitzpatrick
escape me, who have the honor of being genealogist to the
family, and who have studied the MSS. of O'Bull King-at-
Arms to the Milesian Monarchs before they had any arms, or
he could write or read . . . The Fitzpatricks . . . are so an-

cient that the Irish antiquaries affirm that they reckoned many generations before the first man was created.

In similar vein, the cynical Mr. Gilbert put these words in Pooh-Bah's mouth: "I am . . . a particularly haughty and exclusive person, of pre-Adamite ancestral descent. You will understand this when I tell you that I can trace my ancestry back to a protoplasmal primordial atomic globule. Consequently my family pride is something inconceivable."

Again, there was the lyricist, Oliver Herford, who sang sweetly:

> Children, behold the chimpanzee:
> He sits on the ancestral tree
> From which we sprang in ages gone.

Yes, there have been these doubters, these skeptics, these profaners, and for my soul's sake I must confess that I once was one of them. I once laughed at the lines in Bernard Shaw's *Man and Superman,* when Mrs. Whitefield objected: "We can't help loving our own blood relations," and Tanner replied: "I suspect that the tables of consanguinity have a natural basis in a natural repugnance." That sounded so urbane, so sophisticated, so wonderfully worldly.

But as I have matured, as I have grown old and, perhaps, enfeebled, I have changed, I have been converted, I have repented of my shallowness, my delusion, my arrogant error. Actually, genealogy has become for me, not only respectable but desirable. To understand how this is so, Giovanni, you must understand that I have myself become an ancestor and look forward with eager expectancy to being worshiped. Let my younger generations take dutiful and filial and reverent notice!

When, in his fifty-second year, Edward Gibbon had completed his "arduous and successful work" on the *Decline and Fall of the Roman Empire,* he determined to devote his leisure to a review of "the simple transactions of a private and literary life." The result was the celebrated *Memoirs.* In the introductory pages he wrote:

. . . A lively desire of recording our ancestors so generally prevails, that it must depend on the influence of some common principle in the minds of men. We seem to have lived in the persons of our forefathers; it is the labour and reward of vanity to extend the term of this ideal longevity. Our imagination is always active to enlarge the narrow circle in which Nature has confined us. Fifty or an hundred years may be allotted to one individual, but we step forwards beyond death with such hopes as religion and philosophy will suggest; and we fill up the silent vacancy that precedes our birth, by associating ourselves to the authors of our existence. Our calmer judgment will rather tend to moderate, than to suppress, the pride of an ancient and worthy race. The satirist may laugh, the philosopher may preach, but Reason herself will respect the prejudices and habits, which have been consecrated to the experience of mankind. Few there are who can sincerely despise in others an advantage of which they are secretly ambitious to partake. The knowledge of our own family from a remote period will be always esteemed as an abstract preeminence, since it can never be promiscuously enjoyed; but the longest series of peasants and mechanics would not afford much gratification to the pride of their descendant. We wish to discover our ancestors, but we wish to discover them possessed of ample fortunes, adorned with honourable titles, and holding an eminent rank in the class of hereditary nobles, which has been maintained for the wisest and most beneficial purposes in almost every climate of the globe, and in almost every modification of political society.

Accept that statement, Giovanni, accept that declaration of life as a great *continuum,* or return to considerations which you better understand.

A Neglected Bookman:
Calvin Coolidge

WHETHER the abundant evidence is carelessly ignored or, whether there are those angrily resolved to overthrow it, there is no gainsaying the fact that ours is the Age of the Odious Comparisons. Lives are imprisoned by bewildering schedules of imposed priorities and ancient, personal liberties are forfeited to the indignities of tyrannic standards. Ratings enslave the race: performance ratings, experience ratings, financial ratings. Everything, everyone is contrasted and usually unfavorably. There are no freedoms any more. In offices of government, in classrooms, in the back parlors of learned societies, vicious men and malicious women invent maddened measures and apply them to their ignominious fellows. The individual, who once was human being and bore a name, is now only a statistic and, as a statistic, known merely by the plus or minus sign affixed by misanthropic enumerators. Make no mistake about it: the American, once proud and strong and endowed by the Creator with inalienable rights has disappeared into an entry in some tormented table. Unheeded is the Pauline warning: "Know ye not that they which run in a race run all, but one receiveth the prize?" And yet, in our epoch, only one courageous spirit has chosen not to run.

It is time to bring an end to this Age of the Odious Comparisons, for unless it is ended promptly, unless it is utterly obliterated, unless it is repudiated and superseded by reason restored and reason honored, American institutions must surely perish. Already they have been partially destroyed. In literature the wreckers of the Debunker School have publicly burned the superlatives which once enlivened the Republic's pert patrology and today the text is nothing more than a wavering line upon a graph. Not so long ago the *Lincoln Herald,* for example, contained the biography of a politician, formerly esteemed, presented in a series of charts and entitled, *Mr. Lincoln's Light From Under a Bushel.* As a practical demonstration of degraded taste the production is not without interest, but it is fervently to be hoped that the experiment will never be repeated. Recently, a New York publisher has initiated a crusade to translate the forlorn dramatic compositions of a late resident of Stratford into the exciting, colorful, rollicking medium of the modern comic book, complete with intelligible, colloquial captions, and addressed, according to the prospectus, to the edification of not one public but two: "the adult who has read few, if any, solid, substantial books; and . . . the high school student who is seeking an anxiliary [sic] aid to his high school work."

But the decline of the West has been alarmingly illustrated in the Age of the Odious Comparisons by the forebodings of indigenous philosophers. Consider, if you will, such a statement as this, made not so long ago, by William

Penn Adair Rogers, in connection with *Yes We Have No Bananas:*

I would rather [he said] have been the Author of the Banana Masterpiece than the Author of the Constitution of the United States. No one has offered any amendments to it. It's the only thing ever written in America that we haven't changed, most of them for the worst.

Obviously tradition, nice, neat, respectable tradition, cannot survive such odious comparison at the hands of any modern author who, as William Faulkner, having briefly forsaken his cow, recently told a Swedish audience:

. . . writes not of love but of lust, of defeats in which nobody loses anything of value, or victories without hope and, worst of all, without pity or compassion. His griefs grieve on no universal bones, leaving no scars. He writes not of the heart but of the glands.

At his hands, then, what chance for endurance has so frail a thing as reputation? Clearly, reputation has no chance whatever for endurance, until the revolution changes our society, until the revolution re-establishes a sense of greatness, until it comes with adherents stout enough and in such pluralities as to insure a victory. The cause is good. The suffering is great. Recovery is, somehow, possible.

For my own part, I have nobly determined to rescue from detractors and diminishers him who was Chairman of the Board of Trustees of this Shakespeare Memorial Library when it first opened its doors in that April of some three decades gone. His is, in my opinion, the most tragic loss to the Age of the Odious Comparisons for he has been foully betrayed by members of his own lodge, who stole his side arms and turned them straight on him. It was this way:

At Andover, Massachusetts, on May 19, 1928, His Excellency Calvin Coolidge, President of the United States, addressed some forcibly assembled students on the occasion of the one hundred and fiftieth anniversary of Phillips Academy.

The world [he reminded them] will have little use for those who are right only part of the time. Whatever may be the standards of the classroom, practical life will require something more than 60 per cent or 70 per cent for a passing mark.

He spoke those words and they are not, I submit, words which would come readily from one about to flunk. But what happened? He returned to Washington, served out his term, and subsequently proved his own mortality. Then, long after he had entered the paradise reserved for those who had faith in Massachusetts, fifty-five students of American history and government throughout the country got together and compounded a yardstick for the Presidents. Did Mr. Coolidge get, in this examination, a mark of 60 per cent or 70 per cent or better still an A+? Did he pass? I am distressed to report that he did not. Instead he was tagged with a 23 and this Olympian judgment, summarized by Professor Arthur M. Schlesinger: "Of the remaining eight Presidents, six rank below the average without being utter failures. John Tyler and Calvin Coolidge head the list." This, of course, is very shameful, very humiliating, and a little more than monstrous. Professor Schlesinger insists that "the consultants found little difficulty in agreeing upon who were the great and near-great Presidents and which ones failed"; but he admits that "not all [the jurors] indicated their criteria, and it is evident that they could and did use different ones." Certainly their findings are deplorably unscientific and reflect only the predilection of youth for noisy prejudice. Controverting them is Mr. Sinclair Lewis, himself no reckless adulator, who conceded the fact that Mr. Coolidge "fulfilled many of the soundest American ideals, and . . . stands, along with the Ford motor car, the Rev. Dr. William Sunday, and the *Saturday Evening Post,* as the symbol of his era."

It is ridiculous to believe that one who was "symbol of his era" may fairly be pronounced deficient. No, the faults were not of Calvin Coolidge but of the improper points by which he was scored. Suppose, for example, that a more accurate meter had tested his career. Suppose that the fifty-five students of history and government had set out to discover what Presidents have enriched our language or, more specifically, ever said anything worth repeating. To these questions answers are possible and the results (making due allowance for the compiler's inevitable idiosyncrasies) are at least objective. It is necessary only to turn to certain standard works to ascertain them. Burton E. Stevenson's *Home Book of Quotations,* issued in 1949, places Calvin Coolidge in a ninth-place tie with James Abram Garfield where they are surpassed only by Thomas Jefferson, Abraham Lincoln, Woodrow Wilson, Theodore Roosevelt, George Washington, Grover Cleveland, John Adams, and John Quincy Adams. Mr. Coolidge is, in other words, among the elect who have coined our wiser saws and more modern instances.

In the Morley-Everett recension of John Bartlett's

Familiar Quotations, published in 1948, Mr. Coolidge
does not fare so well; there he falls to undisputed thir-
teenth, being superseded by Abraham Lincoln, Franklin
Delano Roosevelt, Thomas Jefferson, the first Roosevelt,
Herbert Clark Hoover, Woodrow Wilson, Grover Cleveland, Ulysses Simpson Grant, Harry S. Truman, John
Quincy Adams, William Henry Harrison, and General
Washington. It would be surprising if scientists with tem-
peraments as unalike as Mr. Stevenson and Bartlett's re-
visers should reach, independently, exact agreement, but
they do join to confirm the fact that Chester Alan Arthur,
James Buchanan, Franklin Pierce, and James Knox Polk
never evoked the faintest echo, and both assign to Mr.
Coolidge a position far above the average. The "symbol
of his era" was a man of few words, but when they
sounded they were memorable enough to attract the lexi-
cographers. This alone is enough to give him stature
among our men of letters.

As a writer of prefaces, the frequency tables indicate
that he held his own with Taft, Wilson, and Franklin
Roosevelt, and was outnumbered only by Theodore
Roosevelt, who must have found a way to write 'em on
horseback. He never produced an English version of the
De Re Metallica, but he recorded in his *Autobiography*
how deeply Cicero's orations held his attention and how
he "translated some of them in later life."

It is, however, as a bookman that his powers have been
most shamefully ignored. An instinctive sobriety, intensi-
fied by presiding over the Eighteenth Amendment, may
have saved him from that deplorable disease, biblio-
mania, which the elder D'Israeli described as "the exquisite inebriation," but, keeping his passion usually

within decorous bounds he, nevertheless, was sensitive to its deranging force. No less an authority on the subject than Dr. A. S. W. Rosenbach once related this revealing episode to the American Antiquarian Society:

> Mr. Coolidge [said the Doctor] was interested in the news of the world. He read of the sale in London of the original manuscript of "Alice in Wonderland" which I had purchased. On my return from abroad in May, 1928, the President asked me to lunch at the White House and to bring along the manuscript. I found that "Alice in Wonderland" was one of his favorite books, that he was interested in Shakespeare, that he liked to own good editions. He asked me details of the first publication of "Alice in Wonderland" and I tried to explain to him that the first edition, issued in 1865, not being altogether to Carroll's liking, was suppressed. "Suppressed?" said the President, "I did not know there was anything off-color in Alice."

Only an intuitive, disciplined, ardent *amateur des livres* could have made so penetrating an observation as that. It combines the most searching literary criticism and a profound scholar's incorruptible incredulity. But Mr. Coolidge's bibliophilism, however characteristic its manifestation, or startling its expression, or fastidiously secreted by its proprietor, was of such a nature as to present itself to partisans not as scandal but as extraordinary virtue.

Among Jeffersonians, it is fashionable nowadays to make preposterous claims in behalf of Saint Thomas. Some go so far as to allege that he was *inter alia* the progenitor of that misguided and misbegotten and mischievous people: the race of librarians. To support their tenuous pretensions, they recall, with lamentable impudence, how he robbed the grave of Francis Bacon, absconding with a division of knowledge which the ghoul applied to the classification of books. Continuing, they insist that he furthered the cause of gentle culture by practicing the mysteries of cataloguing, whereas his exercises in that direction were so ludicrous and bumbling that a later generation has had to do his work all over again and at considerable expense. His courtiers even represent him as a magnificent collector.

Now some forms of folklore may be dismissed as innocuous, but when it is circulated by the sinister to defraud justice and to arrogate to one man the glory due another, its capacities for evil and confusion are unlimited and in restraint of trade. Not Jefferson's but the soul of Coolidge is identifiable with librarianship. Take, for example, the annual accession rate. By his own admission, in the course of more than half a century, the best Mr. Jefferson could do was to acquire exactly 6,487 volumes, magnified in their outward seeming by some grandiose folios; whereas Mr. Coolidge in less than six full years effortlessly accumulated 4,000 wonderfully decorative octavos. But Mr. Coolidge's superiority was exemplified in other ways. Mr. Jefferson squandered his uncertain fortunes in brazenly buying books; whereas, by a resistless affinity akin to gravity, books came to Mr. Coolidge unsought and unsullied by the tainted market place. Mr. Jefferson willfully, stealthily, uneasily concealed his ownership of books by marking them with a cipher cunningly hidden on their signatures; but Mr. Coolidge unembarrassed by earthly possessions caused his name to be wrought in gold upon outside front covers.

Again, Mr. Jefferson, a democrat with aristocratic

tastes and tendencies, was exclusive, finical, dainty in his choices; while Mr. Coolidge, scorning snobbery, gladly naturalized "the huddled masses yearning to be free" in his republic of letters. Finally, Mr. Jefferson let it be known that he sometimes allowed his eyes casually to roam across a printed line, or down a paragraph, or through a text; but the more prudent Mr. Coolidge did his perusing so privately that the Head Usher of the White House was bemused into proclaiming in his notebook the entirely fallacious belief that "Coolidge . . . confined his reading . . . to the daily papers." Mr. Coolidge was, in other words, obedient to the tradition that if a President transgresses beyond the study of Comptroller General's reports, the *Congressional Record,* and musical criticism, he will inevitably invite impeachment.

In reality, the carefully cultivated legend that Mr. Coolidge was separated from the arts by an impassable gulf of prideful peasantry is completely without foundation. Mr. Jefferson once counseled a young gentleman: "A little attention . . . to the nature of the human mind evinces that the entertainments of fiction are useful as well as pleasant." But did he, aside from passages in State papers, extend utility or promote pleasure by himself creating works of the imagination? Mr. Coolidge did, in a graceful contribution to *The Amherst Literary Monthly,* entitled "Margaret's Mist," which concluded with these moving, stirring, unforgettable lines:

Ever since that day when the western sun kisses the rippling lake good night, the mystic cloud so long known as Margaret's mist, appears at the bend over Table Rock to mark the tragic spot and signify the purity of the soul, so long ago gone out beneath its shadow.

Could anything be more sublimely elevating? The prose is simple, supple, and superb. It is nostalgic and sinewy and shaken with tender pulsations. It is experience expressed by one who was master of his craft.

There is something imitative, derivative, self-consciously Lincolnesque and reminiscent of Springfield, in his apostrophe to Vermont—delivered from a train platform many years later: "It was here that I first saw the light of day; here I received my bride; here my dead lie pillowed on the loving breast of our everlasting hills."

But James Barrie must have approved, and may have envied, the perfect phrasing of the inscription which he wrote on a flyleaf shortly after the tragic death of Calvin Junior: "To my friend [it reads], in recollection of his son, and my son, who, by the grace of God, have the privilege of being boys throughout Eternity."

It was in their attitude toward the chroniclers, however, that the differences between Mr. Jefferson and Mr. Coolidge were most marked. Mr. Jefferson regarded them with uniform suspicion and usually with petulant disdain. He dismissed Beverley and Keith as "merely superficial." Henry Lee's *Memoirs of the War in the Southern Department of the United States* was, to him, no more than a "parody." He felt constained to write "antidotes of truth to the misrepresentations" in John Marshall's *Life of George Washington.* John Smith's style was "barbarous and uncouth." William Stith had "no taste."

Mr. Coolidge responded to an opposite impulse. Gamaliel Bradford who wrote of him as "the genius of the average," declared that "as years went on the reading was almost entirely restricted to books of history and government." Mr. Coolidge himself has recorded how his grandmother read aloud to him *The Rangers or the Tory's Daughter,* and *The Green Mountain Boys.* Of his school days at Ludlow he remembered the teachers from whom, as he put it:

I first learned of the glory and grandeur of the ancient civilization that grew up around the Mediterranean and in Mesopotamia. Under their guidance I beheld the marvels of Old Babylon, I marched with the ten thousand of Xenophon, I witnessed the conflict around beleagured Troy which doomed that proud city to pillage and to flames, I heard the tramp of the invincible legions of Rome, I saw the victorious galleys of the Eternal City carrying destruction to the Carthaginian Shore, and I listened to the lofty eloquence of Cicero and the matchless imagery of Homer. They gave me a vision of the world when it was young and showed me how it grew. It seems to me that it is almost impossible for those who have not traveled that road to reach a very clear conception of what the world now means.

It was in this period that I learned something of the thread of events that ran from the Euphrates and the Nile through Athens to the Tiber and thence stretched on to the Seine and the Thames to be carried overseas to the James, the Charles and the Hudson. I found that the English language was generously compounded with Greek and Latin, which it was necessary to know if I was to understand my native tongue. I discovered that our ideas of democracy came from the agora of Greece, and our ideas of liberty came from the forum of Rome. Something of the sequence of history was revealed to me, so that I began to understand the significance of our own times and our own country.

No one can read those lines and quite dismiss them as an idyllic memoir of adolescence. On the contrary, it is necessary to accept them, not in terms of passing fancy and puppy love, but as the persistent passion which it really was. As a matter of fact Clio occasionally returned his burning adoration. The Sons of the American Revolution awarded him "the prize of a gold medal worth about one hundred and fifty dollars for writing the best essay on *The Principles Fought for in the American Revolution,* in a competition open to the seniors of all the colleges of the nation." In the Massachusetts Legislature he found time to absorb *The American Statesman* series, which "cheered him and helped him to understand himself." At the time of his death he was engaged in preparing a condensation of the annals of the United States for incision on the walls of Mount Rushmore.

And yet, Mr. Jefferson, who held them in contempt, has been canonized by successive hordes of historians, while Mr. Coolidge, who furnished them with plentiful materials and esteemed their dangerous enterprises, fared badly at their hands. This may be explained only on grounds of professional jealousy. Where they engaged in idle speculation, he spent himself in less humid pursuits. They sought, these encrusted Procusteans, to dispose of him by comparabilities and he eluded them because he was himself incomparable. Bradford introduced this wholly spurious aspersion: "It does not appear that he read much for pleasure." Why should he? What were the books which were being read for pleasure in the years of his Presidency? They were *The Sheik, Black Oxen, The Sea Hawk, Gentlemen Prefer Blondes, Beau Geste, The Murder of Roger Ackroyd, Trader Horn,* and *Bad Girl.* These were *Mayflower* stuff, suitable for a weekend cruise. But, in the White House he was seldom a hammock swinger and had an honest respect for the Constitution's public welfare clause. William Allen White tells how, when Governor of Massachusetts, he was taken to Emily Dickinson's house and shown one of her manuscripts. He stared down at the paper for a moment and exclaimed: "She writes with her hands; I dictate." When he learned of the Government's purchase of the St. Blasius-St. Paul copy of the Gutenberg Bible, together with 3,000 other fifteenth-century books, for $1,500,000 he was shocked. "I should think," he broke out, "that an ordinary copy of the King James version would have been good enough for those Congressmen."

But despite a popular fallacy, frugality and bookmanship are not always mutually exclusive. I can testify to that. My personal acquaintance with his propensities as a collector began in the fall of 1923, when he addressed an appeal to the Librarian of Congress:

I have [he wrote] quite a number of books on the shelves of the White House that ought to be assorted and arranged. When that is done, there ought to be enough books sent down from the Library to fill out the shelves. If you can, I wish you would send down someone to arrange my books first, and then we can see what other books are needed from the Library.

In response, I was designated as bibliographical stableboy and performed that agreeable but sometimes enervating duty until the Great Engineer terminated the Coolidge tenancy.

In those days, the White House library was housed in the Lincoln study in the east wing of the second floor. The President's desk, flanked on one side by the Stars and Stripes and on the other by the President's flag, was placed between tall windows overlooking the south lawn. Its surface was uncluttered by those gimcracks, knickknacks, and glittering mementos which would one day delight a successor. Above the mantel hung Arthur Keller's dramatic picture of Colonel John C. Coolidge, notary public, standing in the parlor of his Plymouth farmhouse, the gloom partially dispelled by two oil lamps, and administering the oath of office to his solemn son who faced him across a marble-topped table. Opposite, hung Howard Chandler Christy's charming portrait of charming Mrs. Coolidge, bedecked in a red dress, one hand resting on an animal just escaped from Alfred Knopf's colophon. Overstuffed chairs invited relaxation. A chintz curtain across the southwest corner contrived a closet, and seventeen built-in bookcases with glass doors lined the walls.

Gradually the books were arranged in an order which did little violence to the Library of Congress classification scheme, and which Mr. Coolidge found at once practical and imposing. For a time, the *Rebellion Records,* Richardson's *Messages and State Papers,* and other sets as bulky as Migne's *Patrologia* were employed as fillers, but the President's personal collection grew so rapidly that it was soon possible to return these to the Library of Congress. Whenever a dozen or more books were removed from the shelves or when additions would arrive, Ike Hoover would call the Superintendent of the Reading Rooms who, in turn, would put me on a streetcar and send me packing to the Executive Mansion, where I would place shelf numbers in the accessions and tuck them all away. From this continuing physical contact with the collection I came to know something of the works which composed it and the explanation of their provenience. Aside from a lonely Byron, the entire lot seemed to have come into the President's possession *after* he had taken office. In general, their sources were three: the Superintendent of Documents, friends and beggars eager to keep him *au courant* with every activity under the besetting sun, and authors hopeful that in such an asylum immortality would come to the creatures of their minds.

As though assembled to dispel the myth of excessive reticence, a goodly portion of the shelves was given over to the President's public utterances. His reading copies were printed on one side of each leaf only, and in dispro- portionately large type. These measured sixteen and one- half centimeters and were uniformly bound in limp, light blue morocco covers. For the most part they existed in duplicate but their editions were strictly limited. Many were classifiable as State Papers, messages of one sort or another addressed to the Massachusetts General Court or the Congress of the United States; but many others were occasional in nature and were directed to a variety of audiences, among them: the American Association of Advertising Agencies, the American Federation of Arts, the American Association of Museums, Founder's Day at Carnegie Institute, the American Medical Association, the one hundred and fiftieth anniversary of the Declara- tion of Independence, the dedication of a new building for the National Press Club, a Howard University Com- mencement, the International Livestock Exposition, the annual council of Congregational Churches, the Chamber of Commerce of the State of New York, the Daughters of the American Revolution, the National Fraternal Con- gress of America, the Norwegian Centennial Celebration at the Minnesota State Fair Grounds, and a "visiting dele- gation" of Labor Men. The imprint of the Public Printer appeared most frequently on these orations, but a few were the product of private presses and mistresses of the touch system. They constituted an elegant array, and paralleled in their diversity the exertions of the Prince of Wales.

A question has been raised from time to time as to whether the White House is a human habitation or a kennel. Ike Hoover set down his wonder in his *Random Notes:*

Most all Presidents [he wrote] have dogs, some more— some less. The habit seems to be growing as time goes on. Each administration seems to have more than the previous one. By the time the Hoovers came, a special kennel had to be built and a man detailed from the Army to look after them. At this writing [about 1930] there are nine members of the select dog class on the premises. They range from a small black poodle called Tar Baby to a massive wolfhound named Shamrock . . . by comparison, about like a pin and a loco- motive engine.

Mr. Coolidge had not been immune to the fashion. In- deed, it is almost possible to see a resigned shake of his head as he recalled in his *Autobiography:*

A great many presents come to the White House, which are all cherished, not so much for their intrinsic value as because they are tokens of esteem and affection. . . . I have a beauti- ful black-haired bear that was brought all the way from Mex- ico in a truck, and a pair of live lion cubs now grown up, and a small species of hippopotamus which came from South Africa. . . . We always had more dogs than we could take care of. My favorites were the white collies, which became so much associated with me that they are enshrined in my book- plate where they will live as long as our country endures.

The connection between an *ex libris* and the national survival is a little obscure, but in August, 1925, Frank W. Stearns wrote to the Librarian of Congress:

I have had it in mind for some time to have prepared a proper book plate for the President, which he can use in his own personal library.

I wonder if you can tell me who is the most competent man or woman to furnish a desirable design and have it executed.

Perhaps you will make some suggestion as to what should be on the book plate, and any help you can give me I shall very greatly appreciate.

Herbert Putnam replied: "My own personal inclination is rather for armorial plates than for those attempting pictorial compositions." As artist, he recommended Sydney L. Smith, whose services were promptly retained. Unfortunately, Mr. Smith was prevented by illness from completing the design, and the commission was turned over to Timothy Cole who produced a woodblock containing the Plymouth homestead, a fence, a fishing rod leaning against a tree, a bait basket, a bust of General Washington, the flag of the United States, a cheerful banderole, and, squatting in the foreground, those immortal collies; in other words, a crowded "pictorial composition."

Certainly man's best friend ran everywhere in the Coolidge library. There was Mrs. Wagstaff's *Bob: the Spaniel* and Mr. Ollivant's *Bob, Son of Battle;* Edward Axtell's monograph on *The Boston Terrier;* Cecil Aldin's *Dogs of Character;* John Taintor Foote's *The Pocono Shot;* Albert Payson Terhune's *Treve;* and *"Yel,"* the Memories *of a Happy Dog.* There was even Francis Thompson's *Hound of Heaven.*

In another sense the Coolidge library was an ink-filled aquarium. In addition to a Dwiggins-designed copy of Izaak Walton's classic discourse on "the contemplative man's recreation," that piscatorial paradise rippled with such strikes as William C. Vogt's *Bait Casting;* an inscribed copy of Endicott's *Adventures With Rod and Harpoon; the Book of Fishes;* an author's presentation of Charles Southard's *The Evolution of Trout and Trout Fishing;* William Radcliffe's *Fishing From The Earliest Times;* Bliss Perry's *Fishing With a Worm;* Charles F. Orvis' *Fishing With the Fly;* Richard Sylvester's *Me, My Boy and the Bass;* Frederick G. Shaw's *Science of Fly Fishing for Trout;* George Parker Holden's *Streamcraft;* Edward Ringwood Hewitt's *Telling on the Trout;* George Henry Moore's *Washington as an Angler;* and W. W. Crosby on *Some Western Fishing.*

Of the several departments, the most densely populated was by all odds and by all oddities the Department of the Interior. Indeed, if Mr. Coolidge did not double his weight while escorting prosperity as far as the corner, it was not the fault of the women of America who plied him with their favorite recipes. From all over, they came; from the As You Like It Club, of South Portland, Maine; the Business and Professional Women's Club, of Springfield, Missouri; the Congressional Club, of Washington, D. C.; the Loyal Helpers' Society, of the First Lutheran Church, of Galesburg, Illinois; Court Timon No. 689, Catholic Daughters of America, Buffalo, New York; The Housekeepers' Club, of Pittsford, Vermont; The Methodist Ladies Aid, of Racine, Minnesota; The Bogota Auxiliary, of the Holy Name Hospital, of Teaneck, New Jersey; The Country Club Christian Church, of Kansas City, Missouri; The Woman's Missionary Society, of the Methodist Episcopal Church, South, of Dickson, Tennessee; The Bethlehem Presbyterian Church, of Minneapolis, Minnesota; The Queen Anne Guild, of the Children's Orthopedic Hospital, of Seattle, Washington; The Lady Helpers of the First Congregational Church, of Gannvalley, South Dakota; The Athena Club, of the Woman's Federated Association, of Burlington, Vermont; The Woman's Aid Society of the First Congregational Church, of Malone, New York; The Martha Washington Guild, of Valley Forge, Pennsylvania; The Order of the Amaranth, Incorporated, Aldoniram Court No. 22, of Lyndhurst, New Jersey; The Parents, Alumnae, Students, Faculty, and Friends, of the Veltin School, of New York City; The Guild of the First English Lutheran Church, of Baltimore, Maryland; The Willing Workers Circle of the Congregational Church, of Waukesha, Wisconsin; the Methodist Episcopal Church, of Rockwood, Tennessee; The Student Loan Fund, of Anchorage, Alaska; The Ladies Aid Society, of the Sherman Park English Evangelical Lutheran Church, of Milwaukee, Wisconsin; The Ladies of the Bowen Methodist Episcopal Church, of Chicago, Illinois; The Ladies Aid Society of the Community Church, of Ventnor, New Jersey; The Simpson Chapter of the Epworth League, of Peru, Indiana; The Ladies Aid Society, of the Mount Zion Reformed Church, of Spring Grove, Pennsylvania; The Village Fair Committee, of Downingtown, Pennsylvania; and The Young Ladies Union of St. Paul's Icelandic Lutheran Church, Minnesota, Minnesota. With such numerous collaborators the effect upon the broth could only be disastrous.

Mr. Coolidge did not possess a Gutenberg Bible, but he did own one of the one hundred and seventy-five copies of the *Festschrift* published by the Gutenberg-Gesellschaft at Mainz, in 1925, and the want was further compensated by John Daye's beautiful *Book of Psalmes,* London, 1596, and a copy of the Gideon Bible presented by the Society's president, Mr. Ernest L. Vogel; along with *The Graphic Bible* and *The Runner's Bible,* and William Barnes Goodman's *Business in the Bible.* Among his liturgical works was a copy of the *Booke of Common Prayer with the Psalter or Psalms of David,* which the deputies of Christopher Barker published at London in 1596. Other examples of early printing included William Williams' *Duty and Interest of a Christian People,* Boston, 1736; Aaron Bancroft's *Essay on the Life of George Washington,* Worcester, 1807; Robert Proud's *The History of Pennsylvania in North America,* Philadelphia, 1797; and the first edition, 1804-07, of Chief Justice Marshall's biography of the Father of His Country which had so displeased Mr. Jefferson.

It was custody of these prizes perhaps, which induced diluted Dibdins to welcome Mr. Coolidge to their dubious fellowship. A Mr. and Mrs. Edward G. Buckland contributed A. Edward Newton's *This Book-Collecting Game;* from an unknown source came John Erskine's *The Delight of Great Books;* while Joseph F. Jennings and Richard F. Fuller pitched in Dorothea Lawrence Mann's *A Century of Bookselling: the Story of the Old Corner Book Store.*

It would be agreeable to find support of Mr. Coolidge's broad renown as a Shakespearean among the contents of his library. Unfortunately the testaments are lacking. There was, to be sure, the Daniel V. Thompson edition of *Macbeth*, 1917; the *Songs and Sonnets*, edited by "Golden Treasury" Palgrave and in a special binding; *The Tempest* as illustrated by Arthur Rackham; and Edwin Gordon Lawrence's commentary, *Sidelights on Shakespeare*; but the only unusual item was *The New Hamlet, intermixed and interwoven with a revised version of Romeo and Juliet; the combination being modernized, re-written and wrought out on new-discovered lines, as indicated under the light of the higher criticism by Wm. Hawley Smith and the Smith family; printed from the original manuscript, with text in full, and as first produced when done in action by the Smiths, their own company, under the haw tree, on their farm at the thicket, June 17, 1902.*

For one of his histrionic disposition, it is contradictory and a little disquieting to discover Mr. Coolidge's indifference to the "drayma." Aside from a collected edition of Oscar Wilde's plays; a copy of Shaw's *Saint Joan*, signed by the American cast; and Laurence Housman's *Angels and Ministers*, there was almost nothing. As for players, Otis Skinner spoke for himself in *Footlights and Spotlights;* there was something wistful and long ago in *Wallace Reid: His Life Story,* as related by his mother.

Novels were few. Miss Ostenso, Miss Sinclair, and Miss Cather were there, along with Messrs. Enoch Arnold Bennett, James Boyd, Newton Booth Tarkington, A. S. M. Hutchinson, Percival Christopher Wren, and Irving Bacheller, but on the whole they made an indifferent showing.

The poets, on the other hand, were rather prominent:

Burns wrote not from Kilmarnock but from Edinburgh, and bore a specially printed presentation page from the miniature Mr. Walter Scott; there was *The Janitor's Boy* inscribed by his begetter, Nathalia Crane; Stephen Vincent Benét sat beside *John Brown's Body;* Lizette Woodworth Reese interested herself in *Little Henrietta;* and out of the American past came the rhyme schemes of Emerson and Poe. Carl Sandburg found melodies in *The American Songbag* and William Brown Maloney turned up with *The Chanty Man Sings.*

When it came to cultural co-operation, first place went to the Roumanians. There was, for example, the *Bulletin Dedicated To Her Majesty Queen Marie,* by the Society of Friends of Roumania, in New York; and Mrs. Constance Lily Rothschild Morris had autographed a copy of her glowing experiences entitled, *On Tour With Queen Marie.* As for Her Majesty herself, she had a rather thin time of it in the Coolidge library. She had presented to the President a most beguiling picture of herself, elaborately framed and complete with crest. I first came upon it, lying face downward behind the *Annual Reports of the Smithsonian Institution* and, supposing it to have been mislaid, placed it conspicuously upon the mantelpiece. When I returned a few weeks later it had disappeared again. This time I found it, apparently lost, behind the *Treaty Series* and transferred it to a prominent position on the desk. But again it vanished and again I recovered it from some sequestered spot. Gradually the truth penetrated my dullness: its removal from view was *intentional.* But the basis of the intent has never been made clear to me. It may be, of course, that Mr. Coolidge believed the heavy silver in the frame would present an

irresistible temptation to his visitors or, his gallant spirit
may have shrunk from exhibiting to vulgar gaze the effusion inscribed upon it.

One thing was certain, Mr. Coolidge was perfectly
aware of the Red Menace. Warnings were mustered in
that otherwise pleasant room: Ole Hanson's *Americanism
Versus Bolshevism;* Charles Sarolea's *Impressions of So-
viet Russia;* William Guggenheim's *Industry, Labor and
Bolshevism, With a Prophecy;* Richard Merrill Whitney's
*Reds in America; the Present Status of the Revolutionary
Movement in the United States Based on Documents
Seized in the Raid Upon the Convention of the Commu-
nist Party at Bridgman, Michigan, Aug. 22, 1922, together with Descriptions of Numerous Connections and
Associations of the Communists Among the Radicals, Pro-
gressives and Pinks;* William English Walling's *Sovietism;*
George Popoff's *The Tcheka, The Red Inquisition;* and
a forerunner of the present Committee on Un-American
Activities, *Revolutionary Radicalism, Its History, Purpose and Tactics With an Exposition and Discussion of
the Steps Being Taken and Required to Curb It, Being
the Report of the Joint Legislative Committee Investigat-
ing Seditious Activities, Filed April 24, 1920, in the Senate of the State of New York.*

Because it had been, after all, *his* study and because
Mr. Coolidge was his idolator and, in some degree, his
counterpart, it was easy for the personality of Abraham
Lincoln to materialize upon those shelves. There it was
in all of the general works, current and long out-of-print;
Dr. Barton dedicated his fine new *Life of Abraham Lincoln* to the President which was present in several copies,
and there were such special tracts as *Abraham Lincoln*

The Christian; Abraham Lincoln The Tribute of the Synagogue; Lincoln in the Telegraph Office; and *Abraham Lincoln in Peoria, Illinois.*

This perfection was not, however, maintained throughout the collection. There was, in fact, an abundance of what the pundits call sometimes *curiosa* and sometimes *ephemera* in their frantic effort to avoid *rubbish.* These had a bizarre, a violently disconcerting effect which can only be reconciled in terms of a universal genius. A few examples of these literary waifs may prove the point: *The Annual Report of the American Bowling Congress, Incorporated, for 1923;* the records of the First International Thrift Congress, held at Milan, in 1924, and presented by the Central Benificence Commission Governing the Savings Bank of the Province of Lombardy; Clarence Custer Hubbard's *The Instructor in Garment Cleaning;* William C. DeLapp's *Just Plain Chicken Talk;* Gertrude Gage Jordan's *Love's Perfume;* Bernarr MacFadden's *Encyclopedia of Physical Culture; The Mongelli Scientific Double Balance System of Designing* [being] *A Complete Analysis of the Art of Designing for Men's and Boys' Garments;* Andrew F. Underhill's *The Rhymes of Goochy Goggles and His Pollywog Named Woggles;* Carl J. Mittler's *Sheared Cream of Wit;* Manly Ritch's *Thoughts of a Postman;* and *The Year Book of the United States Brewers' Association* for 1915.

Far less dismaying were the materials on Mr. Lincoln's heir. These ana were both intelligible and readily acclimated. They included the biographies written by Roland D. Sawyer, Michael Edmund Hennessy, Robert Morris Washburn, Edward Elwell Whiting, Eugene M. Weeks, William Allen White, Horace Green, C. Bascom Slemp, and a work entitled *Concentrated New England: A Sketch of Calvin Coolidge,* by Mr. Kenneth Lewis Roberts, who later distinguished himself by producing other historical novels. There were many certificates: a certificate of Mr. Coolidge's election as an honorary member of the Advertising Club of New York; a certificate of his membership in the Old Guard State Fencibles of Philadelphia, a certificate of his membership in Philadelphia's Carpenters' Company. There was a work in one hundred and twenty-two pages headed: *A Collation and Co-Ordination of the Mental Processes of Calvin Coolidge,* edited and compiled by one Robert J. Thompson. There were "documents of personal interest to Calvin Coolidge from the archives of an old New England institution devoted to the protection of families," the Phoenix Mutual Life Insurance Company, of Hartford, Connecticut. An engrossed resolution from the National Association of Finishers of Cotton Fabrics thanked Governor Coolidge for ending the Boston police strike. An engraved invitation summoned him to the twenty-sixth national *sangerfest.* Photographs included the graduating class of Black River Academy, Ludlow, Vermont, in May, 1890; the President standing before the statue of Booker T. Washington; his one and only inauguration, and shaking the hand of Arthur W. Smith, son of the New York Governor. There was a memorial of thanks to the President of the United States for his interest and approval of the living evergreen tree planted in Sherman Square, Washington, D. C., December, 1924, to serve as a permanent national community Christmas tree from the Society for Electrical Development, Incorporated. The Christopher Music Publishing Company, of Du Quoin, Illinois, had supplied M.

Azzolina's stirring *President Coolidge March*. From the
Nile Mission Press, Cairo, Egypt, had come H. Rahmet
Bey's tribute, *President Harding Dead, Long Live Presi-
dent Coolidge,* encased becomingly in limp black leather.

His defamers have united to accuse Mr. Coolidge of a
lack of prophetic instinct. He should, they scream in
strident insistence, he should have seen what was coming.
He should, in other words, have spent his administration
gazing into bowls of crystal and divining the future. They
abuse him for a failure to read the stars. They think they
have discovered a weakness.

This is all and altogether nonsense. Calvin Coolidge
was born with a caul. Coming events were *no* secret from
him. It is with delight, therefore, that I invite the vilifiers
to behold foreshadowings cast by his library. What is this?
This is *Democratic Extravagance in Peace Times*. It is
published by the Republican Party. And what is this?
This is an essay by William Graham Sumner. He has
called it *The Forgotten Man*. What have we here? It is
Margharita Sarfatti's *Life of Benito Mussolini*. What is
this book which Alleyne Ireland wrote and inscribed to
the executive seer? It is *The New Korea*. What is that innocent little volume with a foreword by John Galsworthy
and illustrations by Kurt Wiese, which Edward Bok gave
to the President? It is Felix Salten's story of a deer named
Bambi. It is translated by Whittaker Chambers.

But his demeaners do not stop with falsification. Mr.
Coolidge, they say, should have abandoned the poise ordinarily expected from the leader of a great people. He
should have allowed himself to be frightened and, in
turn, should have scared his fellow citizens out of their
heedless wits. Craven himself, he should have communi-

cated his terror to the electorate, and like old Solomon
Eagle, in the days of the London plague, should have
called for quick and feverish repentence. But the calm
of Calvin Coolidge was inviolate and I am glad of it.

I am glad of it because, in 1927, the roof of the White
House was, in a most literal sense, raised. The Coolidge
family, driven forth by the repairs, spent the Spring at
the Patterson house on Dupont Circle and the summer
in the Black Hills. Then, learning that the work was finished, they returned to Washington on September 9,
without announcing their coming in advance. This im-
petuous advent threw the staff into a tissue of tissies. Ike
Hoover felt that fate and precedent had betrayed him and
had confronted him with the most grievous crisis of a
long and up-to-then decent career. The second floor simply wasn't ready for occupancy, every stick of furniture
having been removed to the cellar for storage. And there
was the matter of the library. . . .

He sent for me to hurry down. When I got there the
day was excessively hot and the library was empty, but
almost right away laborers began to bring in books in
baskets and in trays and to dump them on the floor. I had
to work on all fours, a position not only awkward but
humiliating. I was younger then and still retained, however ruffled, a small semblance of dignity. Sorting several
thousand books from a jumbled heap requires a certain
amount of relaxed concentration which my injured pride
rendered almost impossible. I had not been at it very long
when in came one of the dogs immortalized on Mr. Cole's
bookplate. Whether it answered to Rob Roy or Prudence
Prim, I do not know, but I do know that to me it might
have been Cerberus himself. Seeing another quadruped,

it engaged in a series of antics, face-lickings, and shoulder-pawings which contained tidings of a willingness to play. I did not want to play, but, because the unwelcome intruder belonged to the royal household, I expressed my regrets as politely as I could, and suggested, with utmost civility, that he betake himself to almost any other suburb of Inferno he might choose. He refused to be rebuffed and pretended not to understand. Finally, his improper attentions became so annoying that I was reluctantly obliged to get him out of the way by shying at his ear an unabridged Greek lexicon and slamming the door. This done and breathing heavily, I resumed my crawling on the parquetry. But I had hardly recommenced, when the laborers brought in another ton of books and behind them, for all the world like a caboose, came the intolerable, the unspeakable beast. There was just no getting rid of him and when my self-control had reached the breaking point, I ran downstairs and filed a vigorous complaint with Ike Hoover. Ike explained the deference with which it was necessary to treat the benighted creature, but agreed to do what he could. He ordered me, however, to get along with the work and to finish up as quickly as ever I might. That was out of the question.

Instead, I took a walk around the block in a vain search for composure, but the sun was so unmerciful and the humidity so sodden that I was only partially mollified when I got back. I stood in the doorway and looked across the room. I looked and went suddenly and completely and murderously mad, for the curtain in the corner outlined the form of my insufferable tormentor. I ran across the room, drew back my right foot to propel him with a kick that would drive him through the walls and over the portico and down the Mall and into the Tidal Basin, and throwing aside the curtains to make more deadly accurate my aim I looked down.

I looked down at the President of the United States kneeling before a small safe. He had heard me coming, and when I reached him he pushed back his small straw sailor hat and phlegmatically asked me over his shoulder, "How are you getting on?" I do not remember what I replied, or whether I replied at all, but I have not forgotten the salving kindness of his impeccable imperturbability. Let justice be done for it is due him, and it is high time for the rest of us to repeat Will Rogers' tribute when Calvin Coolidge died: "By golly, you little red-headed New Englander, I liked you."

271

11055 5